Editor-in-Chief and Founder:
    Lyndon H. LaRouche, Jr.
Editorial Board: *Lyndon H. LaRouche, Jr. , Helga
    Zepp-LaRouche, Robert Ingraham, Tony
    Papert, Gerald Rose, Dennis Small, Jeffrey
    Steinberg, William Wertz*
Co-Editors: *Robert Ingraham, Tony Papert*
Managing Editor: *Nancy Spannaus*
Technology: *Marsha Freeman*
Books: *Katherine Notley*
Ebooks: *Richard Burden*
Graphics: *Alan Yue*
Photos: *Stuart Lewis*
Circulation Manager: *Stanley Ezrol*

INTELLIGENCE DIRECTORS
Counterintelligence: *Jeffrey Steinberg, Michele
    Steinberg*
Economics: *John Hoefle, Marcia Merry Baker,
    Paul Gallagher*
History: *Anton Chaitkin*
Ibero-America: *Dennis Small*
Russia and Eastern Europe: *Rachel Douglas*
United States: *Debra Freeman*

INTERNATIONAL BUREAUS
Bogotá: *Miriam Redondo*
Berlin: *Rainer Apel*
Copenhagen: *Tom Gillesberg*
Houston: *Harley Schlanger*
Lima: *Sara Madueño*
Melbourne: *Robert Barwick*
Mexico City: *Gerardo Castilleja Chávez*
New Delhi: *Ramtanu Maitra*
Paris: *Christine Bierre*
Stockholm: *Ulf Sandmark*
United Nations, N.Y.C.: *Leni Rubinstein*
Washington, D.C.: *William Jones*
Wiesbaden: *Göran Haglund*

ON THE WEB
e-mail: eirns@larouchepub.com
www.larouchepub.com
www.executiveintelligencereview.com
www.larouchepub.com/eiw
Webmaster: *John Sigerson*
Assistant Webmaster: *George Hollis*
Editor, Arabic-language edition: *Hussein Askary*

EIR (ISSN 0273-6314) *is published weekly
(50 issues), by EIR News Service, Inc.,
P.O. Box 17390, Washington, D.C. 20041-0390.
(703) 777-9451 ext. 415*

European Headquarters: E.I.R. GmbH, Postfach
Bahnstrasse 9a, D-65205, Wiesbaden, Germany
Tel: 49-611-73650
Homepage: http://www.eirna.com
e-mail: eirna@eirna.com
Director: Georg Neudecker

Montreal, Canada: 514-461-1557

Denmark: EIR - Danmark, Sankt Knuds Vej 11,
basement left, DK-1903 Frederiksberg, Denmark.
Tel.: +45 35 43 60 40, Fax: +45 35 43 87 57. e-mail:
eirdk@hotmail.com.

Mexico City: EIR, Sor Juana Inés de la Cruz 242-2
Col. Agricultura C.P. 11360
Delegación M. Hidalgo, México D.F.
Tel. (5525) 5318-2301
eirmexico@gmail.com

New Paradigm Triumphs at G-20

EDITORIAL

China's Intention Succeeds At the G-20

Sept. 5—The Chinese intention for the Sept. 4-5 Group of 20 summit was spelled out in detail over the past months—to unite the world behind fundamental principles, acknowledging the mounting dysfunction of the existing global economic and financial structures, and institutions, and create a new paradigm based on innovation, to replace them with a new financial architecture capable of directing credit into growth and development in every part of the world.

This intention has been achieved, despite wild lies and misrepresentations in the West, and especially by a humiliated and isolated Barack Obama.

The institutions representing nearly the entire world outside of Europe and the United States, have united behind this vision, which is both coherent with, and indeed nearly identical with that presented by Lyndon and Helga LaRouche over the past half century. Both the BRICS nations—representing directly and indirectly most of the nations of Asia, Africa, and Ibero-America—and the G-77, now representing 134 developing nations, released official statements fully endorsing and identifying themselves with this emerging revolution in world history.

Combined with the similarly historic Eastern Economic Forum in Vladivostok on Sept. 2-3, and the ASEAN Summit and East Asian Summit to be held in Laos over the next three days, these events characterize a new momentum in the history of mankind towards ending geopolitics—i.e., British imperial divisions of the world into warring nations, religions, races, and eth-

nicities—and creating a new system based on the common aims of mankind.

In his press conference at the conclusion of the G-20 today, President Xi Jinping said: "We can no longer rely on fiscal and monetary policy alone" to deal with the crisis. "We envision an all-dimensional, multi-tiered, and wide-ranging approach to innovation which is driven by innovation in science and technology, but goes beyond it to cover development philosophy, institutional mechanisms, and business models, so that the benefits of innovation will be shared by all," Xi said.

The war-mongering Obama blathered about human rights, climate change, and the comatose TPP free trade agreement, even as the western world descends into permanent war, economic disintegration, and social degeneration. But the rest of the world was uplifted by the G-20 vision of mankind's creativity as a basis for creating a world of progress for all—including the United States and Europe, were they to end their failed imperial mindset.

Xi said that the G-20 now sees itself as an instrument that can provide a "new path of economic development" for the world, based on a push for scientific and technological innovation.

The leaders of the BRICS nations, who will hold their annual summit in India in October, met in preparation on the sidelines of the G-20. Their communique stated: "Cognizant of global growth challenges ..., the Leaders underlined the importance of establishment of a just and equitable international order based on international law. The Leaders congratulated and supported the Chinese G-20 Presidency for 2016 and expressed full confidence in the successful outcomes of the Hangzhou Summit. They appreciated the emphasis by the Chinese Presidency on the development agenda. They encouraged G-20 members to strengthen macroeconomic cooperation, promote innovation, robust and sustainable trade, and investment growth. They stressed the importance to foster an innovative, invigorated, interconnected and inclusive world economy to usher in a new era of global growth and sustainable development. They expressed expectation that with the Hangzhou Summit, the G-20 will embark on a new journey for a strong, sustainable, balanced and inclusive economic growth."

Similarly, the G-77, headed this year by Thailand's Prime Minister Prayut Chan-ocha, was invited to the G-20, where he said that the proper agenda for the developing nations was precisely that put forth by Xi Jinping at the G-20—innovation, development, and inclusiveness. He added that "Thailand is ready to serve as a bridge linking the Group of 20's major industrialized economies and the developing economies in the Group of 77."

The agenda for the new paradigm is now in place. The dying British Empire and its satrapies will do everything in their dwindling power to crush it. Now, however, the citizens of the western nations have in sight the model and the structure with which to restore their own nations' historic roles in nation-building, and to create at last a truly global Renaissance. That is our task.

EIRContents

www.larouchepub.com Volume 43, Number 37, September 9, 2016

Cover This Week

The Chinese Phoenix is an immmortal bird that appears rarely, signifying peace and prosperity.

Correction: In last week's issue, on page 9, the head of Roscosmos should have been identified as Igor Komarov.

I. On the Space Frontier

MEGAN BEETS

Krafft Ehricke's Extraterrestrial Imperative and the Far Side of Moon

> "The most important development for humanity to date."
>
> —*Lyndon H. LaRouche, referring to China's mission to the far side of the Moon*

Last week, LaRouche PAC scientific and political leader Megan Beets kicked off a sweeping and stunning dialogue with fellow science team members and the nation at large on the question of why it is urgently necessary for the good of humanity that mankind begin the exploration and development of the far side of the moon. Her initiative extended across two events. What was striking about the discussion was that every question, no matter how technical, was answered by challenging the questioner as to his or her own identity and the future of the human race. Edited transcripts follow. The full transcripts, as well as video/audio of the August 31 *New Paradigm* show and the Sept. 1 *Fireside Chat*, are available at www://larouchepac.com

From the August 31, 2016 New Paradigm *show:*

In the recent period, China has announced that in 2018, two years from now, it plans, for the second time this decade, to land a lander and a rover on the surface of the Moon. But this time, it is planning to land in a place that has seen neither human nor even robotic presence before, a place that we have never ever touched, and that is the far side of the Moon.

A lot of people might not know what that means. Why do we say the Moon has a near side and a far side? Or sometimes people might hear, the "dark side," although that's not entirely accurate. If you look at the first slide [**Fig. 1**], this should be a pretty familiar view to you: This is our Moon, maybe in greater detail than

you're used to seeing it. This is the only hemisphere of the Moon that you have ever seen from Earth; this is the only hemisphere of the Moon that any person, or animal to the extent they look up, has ever seen from the surface of the Earth. Now, why? Why can't we ever see the other side of the Moon from the Earth?

The Moon is in a state that's sometimes called "tidally locked" with the Earth; I'm not going to get into all those details, but in short, that means that the Earth itself acts on the body of the Moon and modulates its spin as it orbits the Earth.

Let's look at an example. In the next slide [**Fig. 2**] you see a diagram of the Earth. This is as if we were

FIGURE 1

FIGURE 2

FIGURE 2

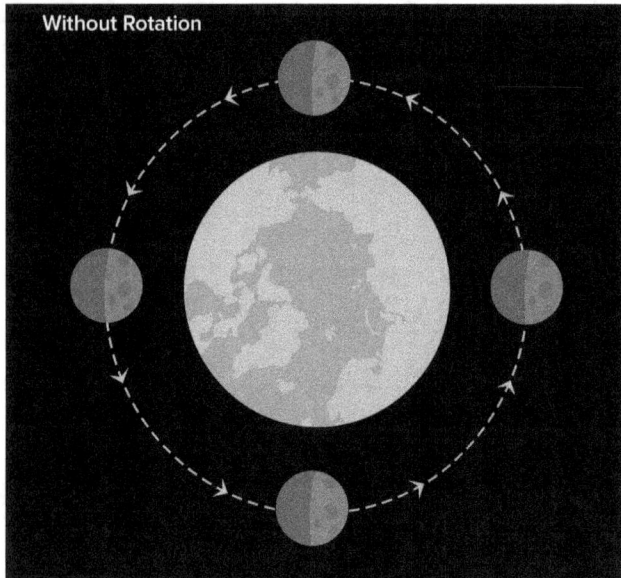

Without Rotation

FIGURE 3

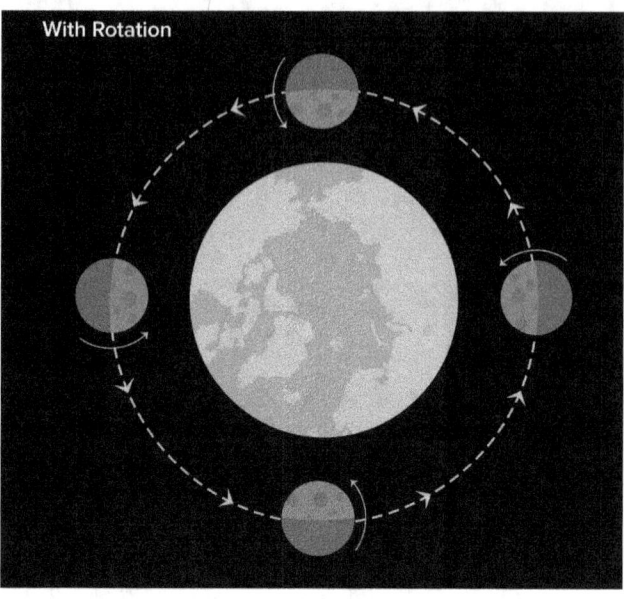

With Rotation

looking down from above the North Pole, and you have the Moon which is rotating counterclockwise. Now, if the Moon merely orbited the Earth, without rotating, then you would see it move from the left side down to the bottom and all the way around its full orbit, and over the course of that orbit people on Earth could see every possible face of the Moon. We would see a 360 degree view, so to speak, of the body of the Moon. But that's not what happens; our Moon does rotate.

So in the next slide [**Fig. 3**] you see the case where the Moon rotates: What you see here is the fact that our Moon, due to the action of the Earth on it, rotates at the exact same rate that it orbits. So starting on the left side, you have the Moon, and as it goes a quarter of an orbit toward the bottom it has also spun a quarter of the way around on its axis. For that reason, the same hemisphere of the Moon is always presented to the Earth.

The Space Age

So for that reason, over the entire span of millennia that humans have been here on this planet, we have only ever seen one face of the Moon. Now the far side of the Moon was not even part of our world, it was something completely inaccessible, unthinkable except to speculation, until, in the 1940s, people such as Krafft Ehricke, about whom I'll say something more in a moment, and others, opened up the space age. They were the first in the 1940s to successfully launch a rocket from the Earth into space, suddenly making it

within the realm of possibility that we could one day see and go to the far side of the Moon.

The space age was opened up, and in October 1957, human beings created the first artificial moon and we put our own moon in orbit around the Earth, and it was called Sputnik. Just one year later, the Soviet Union launched another probe, called Luna 3. Luna 3 left Earth in an orbit that took it swinging around the far side of the Moon.

Luna 3 swung around the far side of the Moon successfully, and you can see in the next slide here [**Fig. 4**] the picture that was taken by Luna 3 of the hemisphere

FIGURE 4

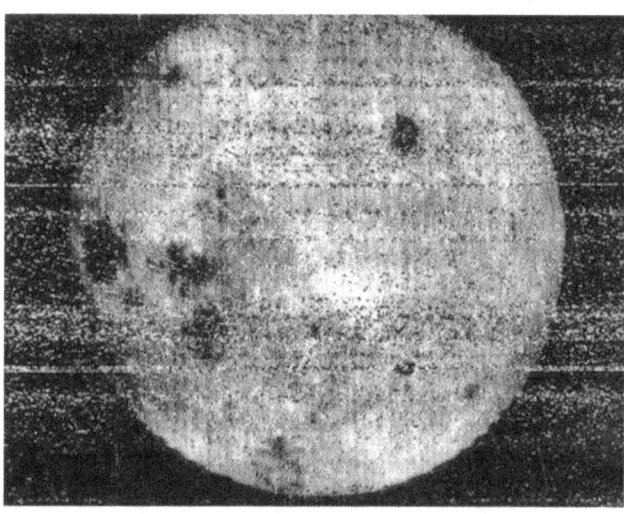

of the far side. I know it's very fuzzy, but you can imagine, and I'm sure some of our viewers may remember suddenly having the first view, ever, of this side of our neighbor, something so close, and yet before so impossible to reach.

Obviously, we've gotten much better pictures since Luna 3. So we've "seen" the far side of the Moon so to speak; we've had images of it. But what many, many people don't realize is that we have never, ever been there. No American, no lander, no Soviet lander, all of these landers that have been sent there over the decades, the Chinese lander—*none* of these have been to the far side. All of them have been on the near side of the Moon. And so the far side, and therefore, the Moon itself, the Moon as a whole, really remains quite a mystery to us. It's something of which our knowledge is extremely incomplete, and it also holds a lot of surprises.

The New Paradigm

Because of where we are in the world strategically—with the collapsing of the trans-Atlantic paradigm, the collapsing of the British Empire and its system of maintaining most of the planet in a state of controlled beasts—the fact that that is over and we're entering a new paradigm with the potentiality of setting up a new system, Mr. LaRouche pointed to China's announcement of this mission as the most important development for humanity to date. I want to read from something that Mr. LaRouche said on the topic in March of this year. He said,

> What is mankind? What are mankind's properties? What is the effect of mankind? What is the role of mankind in respect to the Solar system and beyond? What's that significance? What we're concerned about in order to understand what this reality is, we have to start with the back side of the Moon, which we have not yet seen. We will have some shadow of it, so we'll have to use our minds to understand what the powers are of the human mind which can lead us to the kinds of things we have to consider.
>
> So therefore, we have to accept the process that we are going to operate from the back side of the Moon. We're going to discover what the back side of the Moon is, and from that standpoint, when we've made that experiment successfully, now we will set a new standard for describing what the meaning of mankind is.

Now that's the crucial question: What is the meaning of mankind? What *is* mankind as a species? What is our concept and our understanding of the nature of the creative powers of mankind, and how will that guide our establishment of a new system among peoples, a new system among nations?

That doesn't happen automatically—that creation of a new concept of mankind to govern a paradigm—that's not something which just "happens"; this has to be done willfully and deliberately. I think a lot of people, especially in the trans-Atlantic region, the United States especially, have lost a sense of that. We are not animals, we don't evolve along with the biosphere, we don't evolve along with the whims of the markets. We are a unique species.

The human species, humankind, advances due to the deliberate interventions and actions on the part of genius, on the part of people who have new insight into previously unknown powers of mankind, and an insight into how this changes man's relationship to the Universe. It is individuals such as that and movements such as ours which deliberately fight to establish that notion as a concept among mankind, to establish that as the basis for a new civilization.

Where Were You, When Man Walked on the Moon?

That's really the crucial background, against which people should consider the issue of the Moon, and China's mission and plans to land there in two years. I think that is the challenge, and I think that might not be so obvious to most people. I think it's likely that most people didn't resonate with that announcement that we're going to the far side of the Moon, in the same way that Mr. LaRouche did, and declare that this is the most important issue for humanity now. It just means that Americans, especially, really have to start to rouse themselves out of this slumber, rouse themselves out of this malaise, which then turned into a nightmare that's taken over for the past 40 years, and to imagine where they were, so to speak, mentally, where they were emotionally, before that. Where were they, if they were alive in the 1960s, when man walked on the Moon?

Put yourself in the shoes of a young person in China today. That's the standpoint from which I want people to consider what we're going to consider, what we're going to discuss about the Moon. So with those eyes, of a child or a young person in China, look at the Moon: Now, the Moon is not just a "thing." We tend to look up there and say, "oh, that's a thing, we've been there and then we came back." The Moon isn't an object, or some destination, where we go and then check that off the list. The Moon is a reflection of, and also a clue to processes and principles which govern action within our Solar system and which reflect and can tell us something about the principles which organize our Galaxy and possibly galaxies beyond ours.

LaRouches' Great Friend, Krafft Ehricke

This fact was realized very clearly by Krafft Ehricke. In the next slide [**Fig. 5**], you can see a picture of him speaking to a Fusion Energy Foundation conference in the 1980s. Ehricke was a great friend of Lyndon and Helga LaRouche, and he was first a German, and then an American space pioneer and visionary. As I said, he was part of the team that put the first rocket into space in Germany, and then he became a real foundation and leading visionary of the American space program.

Ehricke was an incredible engineer. He developed the Centaur upper stage hydrogen fuel rocket that we use in virtually every rocket launch today, including the ones that took us to the Moon. Yet Ehricke wasn't just an engineer. He was always thinking about mankind—what does this signify for mankind? What does this potential development, the fact that we could reach the Moon, what does this say about mankind as a species and where we could go? Krafft recalled—somewhat later in life—being twelve years old and going to the movie theater in Germany to see the film "Frau im Mond," which means, "The Woman on the Moon." He went back to see this film eight or ten times as a young man, because it overwhelmed him. He said that, for the first time, he realized that mankind could go to other planets! Mankind had the potential to open up other worlds than Earth.

Krafft saw the Moon in exactly that way. He called the Moon, "Earth's seventh continent," and he saw it as the first step that mankind would

FIGURE 5

EIRNS/Stuart Lewis

take off of the planet to establish himself as a "polyglobal civilization," or a *three-dimensional* civilization. In the last couple of decades of his life, he developed extensive plans for how mankind could develop and industrialize the Moon and establish a permanent colony there.

What drove Krafft was the totally optimistic passion that mankind had no limitations, and I think it's expressed, beautifully and explicitly, in his "Three Laws of Astronautics," which he wrote in 1958, the first of which reads: "Nobody and nothing under the natural laws of this Universe impose any limitations on man, except man himself." If you think about the implications of that, there are no limitations for mankind as long as we don't remain merely on the Earth, as long as we're fulfilling our potential to colonize other worlds. That means that even though mankind may have first appeared on Earth—mankind began

FIGURE 6

on Earth—we are not a terrestrial species, and that comes with a certain obligation to all of us.

The Far Side

So, turn back to looking at the Moon, and turn back to its far side. We've already seen the first picture from 1959 of the Moon's far side. Nine years later, as you can see in this slide [**Fig. 6**], human beings went there. We didn't land there, but the Apollo 8 mission took people to the Moon for the first time, and they orbited around the far side and took this among many other pictures of the Moon's far side. Only a mere eight months after the Apollo 8 mission came the Apollo 11 mission, with mankind's famous first steps on the Moon. The Apollo 11 mission was followed by five other missions which landed people on the Moon, who explored the Moon, who performed physical experiments on the Moon, who drove a little buggy on the Moon, gathered samples of rocks, of dust, of different things they could find to bring back to Earth.

What we have gained from those samples is incredible, and it's such a small sampling of our neighbor, but what we've learned over the last 40 years from those samples, the last of which came back in the 1970s, is absolutely incredible, and we keep making discoveries with this diminishing store of samples—such as that there is indeed helium-3, the fusion fuel, in the lunar soil, something which was hypothesized, but then finally confirmed.

But even with all of this, our knowledge of the Moon is far from being complete, and I think it's illustrated by the fact that the Apollo missions, the astronauts of the Apollo missions, in their explorations of the surface, only covered 5% of the lunar surface; and then you could add maybe a little bit more than that with the Chinese probe and a couple of Russian landers. So we've explored 5% of the surface and all of that was on the near side.

The last Apollo mission, Apollo 17, was launched in 1972. Three more Apollo missions were planned, Apollos 18, 19, and 20. They were cancelled even before the end of the sequence of Apollo missions that did fly. But there was a certain discussion within NASA and particularly within the astronaut corps itself that at last one of those missions should be a far-side mission. We need

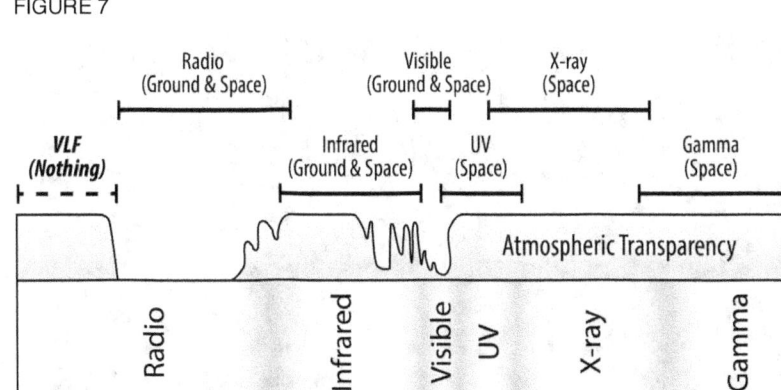

FIGURE 7

Which wavelengths of the electromagnetic spectrum are visible or detectable from Earth's surface, and which are blocked by the atmosphere? The horizontal bank marked Atmospheric Transparency shows, for example, that very low frequency (VLF) radio waves cannot be detected, nor can gamma and x-rays, and some other frequency ranges are partially or wholly blocked.

to keep pushing the boundaries and go to the far side, open up new questions, find new ironies to counterpose to what we've discovered on the near side.

A far side mission, landing on the far side, why didn't we just go there? Why didn't we just go for the biggest goal? Actually it's quite difficult to land and operate on the far side of the Moon. Why? The main reason is that, as we saw, you can't see the far side of the Moon from Earth and people on the far side of the Moon will not see the Earth either. That means that all lines of sight to the Earth are blocked, which means in turn that all radio communications to and from the Earth are blocked from the far side. So that provides a certain amount of difficulty and poses obstacles to be overcome to operate over there.

You have to work with that, obviously. One thing that has been proposed and will be done by the Chinese, is to launch a satellite which will be stationed in an orbit at an adequate distance behind the Moon, and which will be able to see and communicate with both the Earth and the far side, and can act as a relay for communications.

Viewing the Rest of the Universe

There are obstacles, but if we think of being on the far side, and instead of thinking about the the obstacles to communication with Earth, to operating with Earth, coordinating with Earth, and orienting to Earth,—if we think instead of turning around, turning away from Earth, and orienting out toward the rest of the Solar system, toward the Galaxy, toward the different galax-

FIGURE 8

**Hercules A Galaxy
Optical Image**

An image of the Hercules A galaxy (center) in the visible wavelengths.

FIGURE 9

**Hercules A Galaxy
Radio Image**

The Hercules A galaxy in radio wavelengths, disclosing a dramatic pair of gas jets. Many features and objects seen in visible light do no appear.

ies we might be able to see, toward doing astronomy from the surface of the far side of the Moon, well, that radio communication blackout from Earth actually becomes a really wonderful thing!

At this point, Megan discusses the immense possibilities for observing the rest of the Solar system and the Universe beyond, with telescopes that can detect, from the far side of the moon, wavelengths which cannot

be seen through the Earth's atmosphere [**Fig.7**]. *This section is better viewed on the video at larouchepac.com* [**Fig. 8, Fig. 9**], *as is what follows, the elaborate plans for China's 2018 Chang'e 4 Mission, including China's invitation to the world to use its communication satellite and join its mission.*

A New Leap for Mankind

What you are seeing is China in a process of taking a new leap for mankind—and it is for mankind. It has been very explicit about this. This is not for Chinese glory. This is for the advancement of man. And this is where humanity was headed under the space program in the United States and internationally.

I do want to just leave it there, but just to underscore, this is really the potential before us, and this far side of the Moon is not just someplace we're going to go and stick a flag and then cancel our space program. This is the revival of the completely optimistic process that was cut off in the 20th century, that was further cut off by Obama, and the Chinese are opening the door again. And they're opening the door to those questions that LaRouche laid out, in what I read: What is mankind? What are the properties of mankind? What is the effect of mankind as a species? This is what we can decide that we want to establish as the mission orientation of the new paradigm. And that's what China is leading, and Americans should get excited about it and make sure the United States joins that.

During the discussion, Liona Fan-Chiang noted that Mr. LaRouche has always pointed to the space program as a defining feature of all the other things that China is doing, and that it's not a separate subject. It's not that you do this, and you do that, and you also put up an Internet network and whatever; it's not a combination of things for your economy. But it's a declaration of intention: You say, "OK, we're going to develop mankind," and then, "well what's necessary for that? People need to not be starving. People should not be in Third World conditions; they need to be collaborating, and so on, and you build the steps from above.

Megan responded, We're going to develop mankind; actually that's quite provocative. According to today's standards in the trans-Atlantic, you can't say that. You can't declare that you know where mankind should go: The markets determine that. Even if people say, "that's silly," I think most people think like that; most people have let themselves become assimilated into that kind of mindset and it's imperialism.

And that's not what man is. Man isn't an animal. We don't have to wait for nature to do something to us; we create nature. We create new principles when we have an insight into the discovery of something that's true about the Universe. How can we make that happen on purpose? How can we organize all of our activity, as a species all over the planet, with coordination between nations, to make that happen on purpose, and to make it happen more often? It's incredible: No other species can do that. How the Galaxy operates, we still don't know. But then we should also recognize there's probably stuff we haven't even thought of yet, because the whole history of this is a history of surprises. It would be a surprise if we did not get surprises.

A 'Far Side' Chat About the Moon

The following day, Sept. 1, Megan kicked off the weekly LaRouche PAC Fireside Chat with a provocative challenge for listeners to imagine what could have been.

I want to start by asking everybody on the phone here and listening over the Internet, to imagine something. I want you to imagine that it's not late summer of 2016, but imagine that it's late summer of 1986, thirty years ago, and you have just received the news that Expedition Ares, NASA's first manned mission to Mars, has successfully landed. That means that the first human being ever, is about to take her first step on the surface of the red planet.

Now, imagine what that would have meant over the fifteen or so years prior to 1986, the time since the 1969 Moon landing. It would have meant that, instead of the cancellation of the Apollo program, instead of the downsizing of NASA and the layoffs, instead of the shutdown of industry, instead of the takeover by Wall Street, instead of all that, we would have spent those 17 years expanding our presence on the Moon and in lunar orbit.

We would have just begun to build an orbiting space station around the Moon that would house scientists, engineers, and construction workers; we would have established several scientific stations on the surface of the Moon where scientists could go for temporary periods to do astronomical observations and geological work. Some of those science stations could have been on the far side of the Moon, which is where the Apollo 18, 19, and 20 crews would have landed. We would have just set up the first of what would be many automated mining stations on the Moon to begin to utilize lunar resources, and we would have had regular trips to and from Earth's orbit to lunar orbit.

We also would have sent that Expedition Ares crew to Mars, not on a regular chemical rocket, not on the kind of rocket that took people to the Moon. We would have sent them there on a nuclear rocket, meaning that it took them weeks to get there, rather than months. Imagine all of that.

Not a Fantasy

That is not a fantasy. Those were the plans of many of the people inside of NASA and in the space program generally who were the ones to take the leadership to put us on the Moon. That was the outlook of people coming off of the great achievements of the 1960s. Now imagine where we would be today, if that had been our history in the 20th Century, if the United States had not given up on that path, if we as a nation had not given up on what that represents about the nature of mankind.

Now, I want you to imagine something different. Imagine it is the late summer of 2007, which is probably a little bit easier for some of you; so it's late summer of 2007, and you are a young person in China, and China is going to the Moon. In less than two months, a rocket will leave the launch center in China and take a little satellite and put it in orbit around the Moon. That satellite's name is Chang'e 1, and that little satellite is going to orbit the Moon and send back photographs, scans of the surface, and all sorts of data to the people on Earth.

Yutu

Now that is not a fantasy, either. *That happened.* That is China's very recent history. Since then, not only has China developed a very robust manned space program, putting people into space and building a space station, but China has sent three more robots to the Moon: It sent another orbiter, and in December 2013,

FIGURE 10

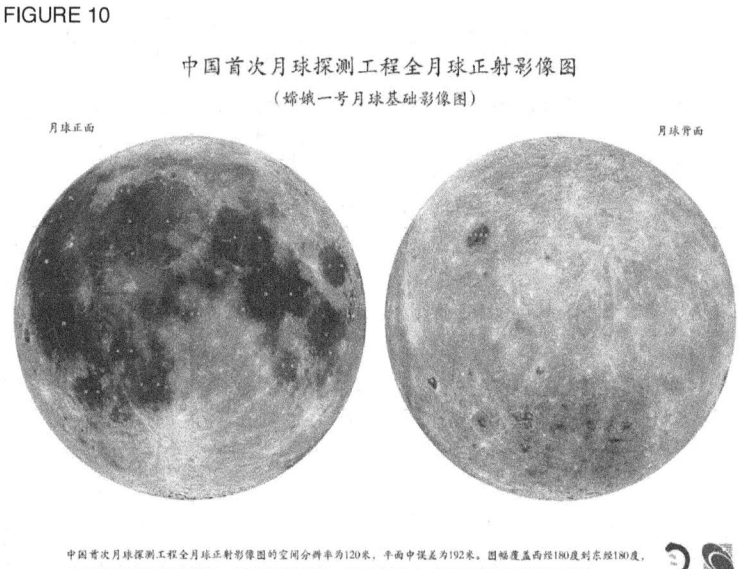

中国首次月球探测工程全月球正射影像图
（嫦娥一号月球基础影像图）

月球正面

月球背面

中国首次月球探测工程全月球正射影像图的空间分辨率为120米，平面中误差为192米。图幅覆盖西经180度到东经180度，
南纬90度到北纬90度之间的范围，图幅左边为月球正面，右边为月球背面，采用正轴等角35度墨卡托投影。

Hemispheric views of the Moon. The far side is on the right.

FIGURE 11

CE-1全月球假彩色地形地貌晕渲图

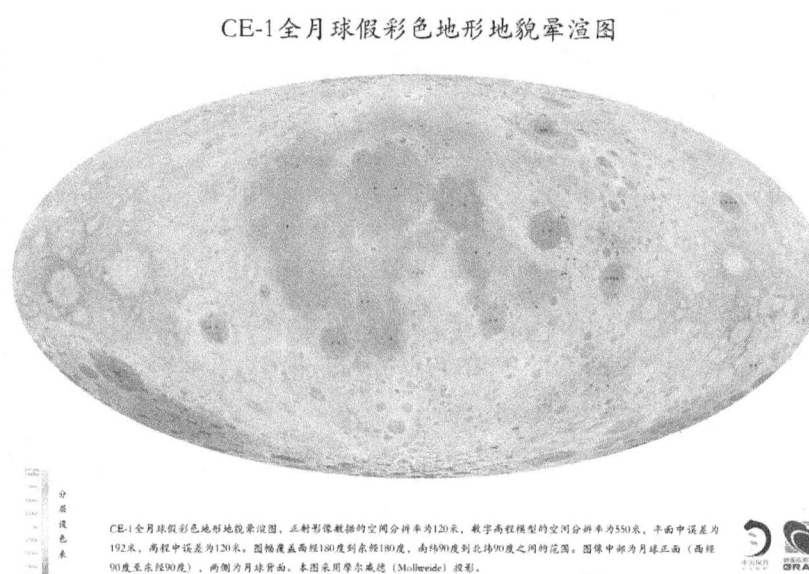

分层设色表

CE-1全月球假彩色地形地貌晕渲图，正射影像数据的空间分辨率为120米，数字高程模型的空间分辨率为550米，平面中误差为
192米，高程中误差为120米，图幅覆盖西经180度到东经180度，南纬90度到北纬90度之间的范围。图幅中部为月球正面（西经
90度东东经90度），两侧为月球背面。本图采用摩尔威德（Mollweide）投影。

A topographic map (Mollweide projection) of the entire surface of the Moon, combining images taken by Chang'e 1.

China sent the Chang'e-3 lander and its little companion, its rover named Yutu, and they landed on the lunar surface. This is the first time in *40 years* that anyone has landed anything on the lunar surface.

Another one of these little robots was sent from Earth; it swung around the back side of the Moon, and

it returned to Earth again, the first time that man has returned anything to Earth from the Moon in 40 years. That happened. Next year, in 2017, China will send its fifth mission to the Moon, and this little robot will land on the surface. It will sample lunar dust, lunar rocks, lunar materials, and will lift off from the surface and will bring these samples back to Earth—again, the first time any sample has come back from the Moon in *40 years*.

The year after that, in 2018, two years from now, China will send a little robot to do what *no country* has *ever* done, and that is to land on the *far side* of the Moon., the side of the Moon that never faces Earth, ever [**Fig.10, Fig. 11**].

That side of the Moon, the far side, is really a mystery to us. It's very, very different from the side that faces Earth, the near side of the Moon, in many different ways, and we don't know *why*. There's something about the process of the Moon that has created this completely fascinating asymmetry, in the structure of the Moon and in many other features, and we have no idea why. The far side of the Moon is also an extremely desirable place to be for astronomy. We'll be able to look out at the Solar system and the Galaxy, and at other galaxies, and see them from the far side of the Moon, in a way that we *cannot* see them from Earth.

Leading the Cause of Mankind

In taking this leadership by doing something which is a first, ever, for mankind, China will begin to open up some questions and begin to answer some of the questions as to the mysteries that the far side of the Moon can reveal to us. Mr. LaRouche has said repeatedly that what China is doing, what it plans to do with the far side of the Moon, is one of the most important things occurring within humanity today, and people have to focus on that. China, in taking the leadership to pioneer a new state for mankind.

Up to this point, the United States, which once had

that kind of identity, has lost it. We have lost our connection to that. We have lost our *identity* that we had in that. It's almost as if a state of amnesia has come over the people of the United States, and we have forgotten what it is to be human. We have forgotten that mankind is a species of perpetual progress.

That's really the mission and that's where we have to set our sights as these incredible developments—occurring over this weekend and into next week in Asia, especially around the G20 Summit—take place.

I will leave it there and we can go to questions.

Freedom from Deductive Thinking

To a question on tidal locking, by which the Earth controls the Moon, Megan responded that the question reflects a mechanistic view of the interactions of the bodies, and that the larger point is that—

as this imperial system crumbles, we can begin to free ourselves, especially in the trans-Atlantic, from the scourge of Bertrand Russell, mathematical thinking, deductive thinking, the idea that man's mind can't actually know anything, and all we can do is describe the effects of things. The more we begin to free ourselves from that, the more we'll have the potential for future geniuses to hypothesize principles that we are not even thinking of, that we have blinded ourselves to, that are actually acting on and organizing the structure and processes of solar systems and galaxies.

Maybe that's a more general comment on what you're saying, but I think that it really is a beautiful thought that future generations will be freed from this kind of mental darkness, that we've suffered under and science has suffered under in the 20th Century. And that will certainly be led by the space program.

Krafft Ehricke

In response to a comment by a caller fascinated by the idea of Krafft Ehricke, that if the Creator wanted mankind to explore the Universe, he would have given us a Moon, Megan replied:

Krafft Ehricke is absolutely the right reference point. Ehricke was always thinking deeply about the nature of man, not just a person, but the nature of mankind as a species. We are unlike any other species on the planet because human beings are not animals. We don't evolve into the future because of biological evolution; it doesn't happen that way. We evolve because of willful, discontinuous leaps upward in our powers which are the result of creative discoveries. That was Eh-

ricke's understanding of man, and that led him to the conclusion that mankind was not supposed to stay on Earth; mankind was supposed to expand from the Earth, to begin utilizing the resources in our Solar system.

He had a really beautiful image of the Earth as a ship which was traveling in the convoy of the Sun. The Earth was the most luxurious of the passenger liners, while the other planets he compared to freighters. They carried all of the resources that we might need. His idea is that mankind is an extraterrestrial species; we have an extraterrestrial imperative.

The beautiful thing about Krafft Ehricke is that he was a visionary. He saw, and in the certain sense of that term, he saw into the future what mankind must become. But he also did the work and laid out the plans of how we might do that. He spent the last decade or more of his life putting together very detailed plans for how we could colonize the Moon and start to industrialize and utilize the resources of the Moon.

But just having this image of Ehricke and his insistence that there were no limitations for mankind, is really the right view.

'Finite But Unbounded'

To a question about Einstein's comment that the Universe is "finite but unbounded," Megan said,

It came from Einstein's work on relativity, considering the shape of space of the Universe. I can't say too much more than that on what Einstein's conception of it was, but in terms of LaRouche's conceptions, what does it mean that the Universe is finite but unbounded? I think it was about seven or eight years ago that LaRouche said, it's better to say that the Universe is infinite but bounded, which is a very closely related idea, and I think what you want to think about is the real nature of the human mind. This is something that people don't spend enough time thinking deeply about: What is the human mind? The human mind makes discoveries, and the discoveries of these principles that are made by geniuses, they don't come from the past, they don't come from deduction. They come from "out of the blue," so to speak.

What is it about the human mind that can actually tap into and bring into existence within the mind, conceptions which didn't exist before, and these conceptions of the human mind—for example, the discovery of Einstein, for example the discoveries of Johannes Kepler, his notion that the planets are moved by *a physical power of the Sun*—these things are formed within the human mind, and yet they correspond to the actual Universe.

This is not something which comes from the senses. It does not come from description. It comes from the same capacity of the human mind that great musical composition comes from.

These Discoveries come from the same capacity that great poetic ideas come from. So what is that mind?

That is what is limitless, that potential to overturn what the human mind was and could do before, and establish something completely new, a completely new meaning of the human mind, new powers of creativity that surpass what came before. That is what is unbounded in Einstein's sense, or infinite in LaRouche's sense.

Cancel Wall Street

In answer to a question on how we can fund the space program when we have so many problems in this country, while China does so because they don't care about their people, Megan replied,

We can, and you ask why we can't bring the space program back—we can. The way we do it is, we cancel Wall Street and we fire Obama. That's how we do it. [Caller laughs.] You need the money for NASA? You cancel Wall Street. You know, why have we gone along with the idea that there are trillions of dollars for the Wall Street *criminals* and people get demoralized and say, "Well, I guess we don't have any money for our space program." Cancel Wall Street! Put them through bankruptcy, reinstate Glass-Steagall. Get our credit system back!

We had a credit system. *Money* has a completely different meaning. Older people may have memories of this—the meaning of money has been completely transformed and degraded over the last 40, 50 years by this Wall Street system. Money has no inherent value! There's no lack of money. Where do we get money? We make it! We just make the money we need, but the problem is value. With the Wall Street system today is the age-old system of empire and they loot. There's a limit to how much you can loot, and kill, and suck the blood of the population. That system actually destroyed the existing value, the current physical wealth and value, but more importantly it destroyed the potential for the creation of future value.

The space program did the opposite. The investment in bringing into being of new discoveries, breakthroughs in principle, which tell us that the Universe is different than we thought—and these principles lead to new powers, new capabilities of machining, exponential growth in the productive powers of our workforce—that creates wealth. That's the proper meaning of wealth, it's the potential of the human mind to make these breakthroughs. The space program is anti-entropic.

China recognizes that. People have a little bit of an outdated idea of China. The current and recent administrations in China have made a complete, 180-degree turn in their vision for China. What we have seen over the past couple of decades is that China has brought 600 million of their people out of poverty! The idea of China today is to finish the job by creating more high-tech urban areas, high industry, high-skilled urban areas, and to connect these with tens of thousands of miles of high-speed rail. You talk about a government that cares about its people, China has built over 10,000 miles of high-speed rail in the past decade—and we have built none. China is different from what most people may have been told, or may remember from times past, and it has surpassed all other countries in the world in this respect.

FIGURE 12

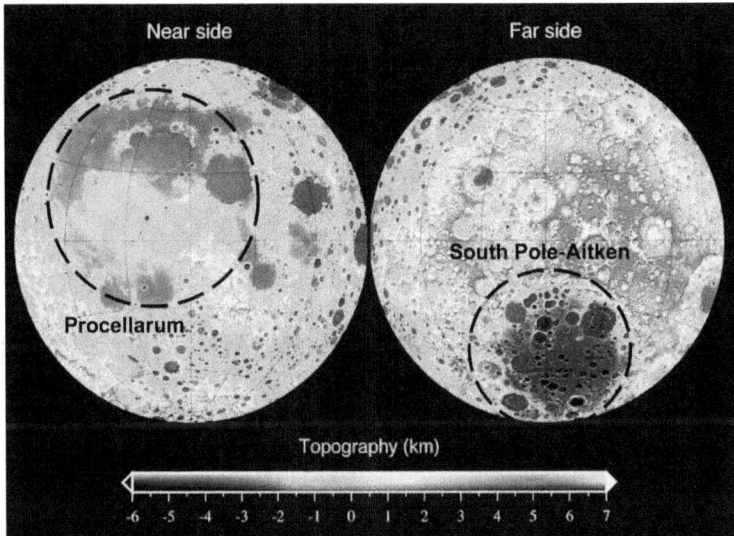

Topographic map showing a large, deep region on the near side and a much deeper region, the South Pole Aitken Basin, on the far side.

FIGURE 13

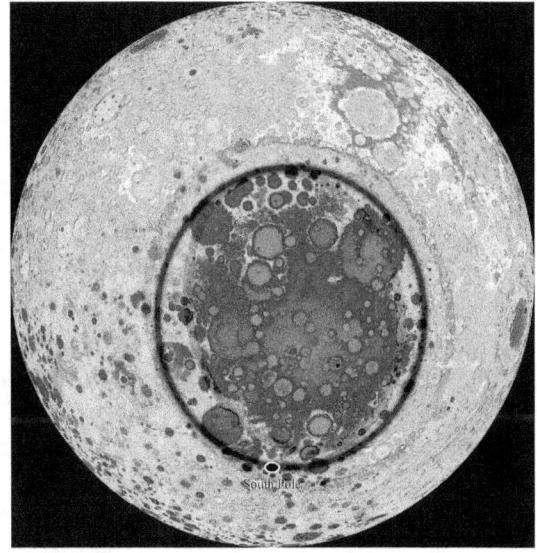

Enlarged view of the Aitken Basin, the largest, deepest crater on the Moon.

Craters on the Moon

Someone asked about the craters on the Moon that are so deep that they get no sunlight. Megan answered,

There are some very interesting features on our Moon which are what the questioner described [**Fig. 12, Fig. 13**]: Craters where the deeper part has never been exposed to sunlight, and these are craters which are near the poles. Which means that they remain at very, very low temperatures. We don't know what kinds of materials are in there; we think that it is possible that gases and materials that go back billions of years to the formation of the Moon could be trapped in them because there has been no evaporation. The Moon is a very tantalizing place to go and study.

But that question just brings up the whole issue that, the Moon is so close—it's a quarter of a million miles away—it's so close, and yet we know almost nothing about it. We need to study the Moon, not from the standpoint of sitting here on Earth and saying "Oh, great, we know that." But we have to study the Moon from the standpoint of letting our activity on the Moon change mankind. Let these questions and challenges to the way we think the Universe works, and let the challenges to our own powers in terms of what we can achieve and make happen—let them transform man-

kind and turn us into a species of a higher order. I think once we take that on, in the way that China is taking it on, as an international effort, I think, 30, 40, 50 years from now we will be a very different species than we are today, and that's something we can be completely optimistic about.

In closing, Megan returned to the main theme.

Act Right Now

The main point is that we are a creative species; there are no limitations. We have an incomparable, magnificent opportunity presented to us, and the developments in Asia are really forging a new future for mankind. It is a future which is unstoppable. Obama and the British cannot stop it. They can start a world war, and that would certainly slow us down, but a new paradigm is coming into existence for man. We in the United States, and especially we in the LaRouche movement, have a lot to offer. We who are around the thinking of Lyndon LaRouche have an indispensable role right now. LaRouche is a genius, and his insights into the nature of the human mind must play a role in the formation of policy and our own outlook on what we want mankind to become. That should be the mission of everybody on this call. And if that's your mission you had better act right now, to make sure that we win.

China Is Leading Mankind in Space

by Marsha Freeman and William Jones

Man is a being of high aspirations.
—Shelley

Sept. 3—China is in the midst of a broad-based, multi-decade space exploration program, which will bring major scientific discoveries, and with them, many other benefits to mankind over the coming decade, as Man realizes his true nature as a cosmic species. China's space initiatives dovetail with its goal of creating a knowledge-based society, where economic progress is the outcome of breakthroughs in science, and their applications through innovation in new technology.

Although China did not first enter space until the 1970s, the nation now has underway short-term manned missions to carry out scientific experiments in low Earth orbit; deep-space robotic exploration missions to the Moon; space science observatories; and an array of applications satellites. On the agenda are a long-duration manned space station; challenging lunar missions that will break new ground in science; space science

satellites for the exploration of the Universe; and the application of space technologies that will enable implementation of the Great Projects of the New Silk Road.

The "New Silk Road," or "One Belt, One Road" initiative, put forward by President Xi Jinping in 2013, is engaging 60 nations, from China's Asian neighbors, through Central and Eastern Europe, to nations in Western Europe, in great infrastructure projects, and new development corridors. Through this program; through the new multilateral financial institutions to fund great projects, like the AIIB and the New Development Bank; and through its own national innovation-driven economic development projects, China is at the center of the mobilization to finally replace the bankrupt postwar Anglo-American financial system, in order to create a global transformation to a growth-based new world order.

Hostile observers criticize China's space program for allegedly competing with other developing space

China National Space Administration

The goal of China's space program is to create a space-faring civilization, that meets the scientific and engineering challenges of exploring the Solar System and deep space. China's space station, seen here in a artist's rendering, will be the base from which mankind will venture forth to explore.

powers, such as India; for only repeating what the United States and Russia have already accomplished; and as a secretive effort, run by a "Communist" regime, closed off from the rest of the world. None of that is true. Either they make these claims out of ignorance, or, more often, in a conscious and determined effort to try to undermine China's emerging leadership role in space exploration, ahead of a former U.S. "super-power," controlled by a former British Empire, which have both seen their international stature in science and technology, along with their productive economies, severely eroded over the past two decades.

Qian Xuesen, became the "father" of China's rocket program, after having been deported from the United States. Here, he is teaching in California before returning to China.

The civilian Chinese space program had a later start than those of the other nations, such as the United States, the Soviet Union, Western Europe, and Japan. But China does not measure itself, or determine its schedule, based on the activities of others. There is no Chinese "space race." Missions are planned, and are executed when they are ready. Each program, such as in manned space and lunar exploration, proceeds through a progression of increasingly-difficult steps, towards a defined goal. Successes once won are not repeated. Each mission poses new challenges.

China is in the process of virtually remaking its civilian space capabilities. A new, more efficient launch complex has been inaugurated on Hainan Island. An entirely new family of launch vehicles is under development. The Long March 5 will have the capacity to orbit future 20-ton space station modules, and eventually the heavy-lift Long March 9 will take men to the Moon.

And, in the past few years, China has taken a dramatic step to open its space program to international collaboration, and boasts cooperation agreements with over 30 nations. But beyond agreements to share technology, now China has also invited other nations to be participants in its once-closed manned space program, offering to accommodate foreign astronauts on its future space station.

The fact that the U.S. space agency has been forbidden by law from manned space cooperation with China since 2011, has been attacked and ridiculed by former U.S. astronauts, policy shapers, and even by NASA Administrator Charlie Bolden. The European Space Agency is already having its astronauts learn Chinese.

In 2022, when the Chinese space station is fully operational, the International Space Station will be nearing the end of its life. Will the United States continue to have a manned space program at all? When the Chinese make major scientific advancements in their lunar program, and plan for manned landings, will the United States continue the Obama policy of selling off the nation's scientific patrimony and future to the "private sector?"

China has invited the rest of the world to join in its global development program, and the venture of Man and his creative intelligence into space.

Inspiring the Space Venture

The world first began to take notice of China's burgeoning space program in 2003, with the launch of Yang Liwei, China's first man in space. But China's interest and fascination with space goes further back.

Readers are probably aware of the shock effect that the 1957 Soviet launch of Sputnik had on U.S. political circles, leading to the initiation of a fast track on space and rocket development in the United States. Sputnik also had its effect on the Chinese leadership. Coincidentally, Chinese leader Mao Tse-tung arrived on his second—and last—visit to Russia, in November 1957, just one month after Sputnik was launched. On his arrival, he congratulated the Soviets for their "great accomplishment that exemplifies the beginning of a new era of humankind's progressive conquest of nature." In advance of Mao's visit, the Chinese and Soviets had signed agreements whereby Russia would assist China in the development of nuclear weapons, missiles, and aircraft.

China also had its own resources as well. Chinese-born Qian Xuesen was a protege of the Hungarian-American aeronautics and astronautics scientist Theodore von Karman at the California Institute of Technology. In November 1943, Qian was one of the founders of the Jet Propulsion Laboratory at the California Institute of Technology. The laboratory became one of the early pioneers of rocketry and ballistic missile technology in the United States.

Qian's accomplishments were so impressive that at the end of World War II, he was inducted into the U.S. military, in order to go to Germany to interrogate the team of German rocket scientists led by Wernher von Braun, who had surrendered to the Americans and were prepared to work with the United States on developing rockets. Rudolph Hermann, one of the von Braun team at Peenemünde, who had designed their wind tunnel, relates his encounter with Qian during his interrogation. "I remember one of them," Hermann writes, "Dr. Qian, von Karman's closest associate, because he had written the paper about the "Pressure Distribution on a Cone in Supersonic Flow." He was the only scientist who had ever written a complete theory [on the subject]. We knew about his theory, because it was published about two years prior to the end of the war. We had used his theory and tested it in our tunnel exactly. I found out that nobody so far had tested Dr. Qian's theory in his country. We did it, because we had the equipment, we had the supersonic tunnel, the scientists and the engineers."

When he was at Cal Tech, Qian was involved with a group of young scientists and engineers that included future rocket-developer Frank Malina, future physicist Frank Oppenheimer, and others who were surreptitiously doing experiments on suborbital sounding (research) rockets. Qian's favorite pastime was listening to Bach or symphonies of Beethoven. And, like many young men

The Dong Feng-1, developed under Qian's guidance, seen here, was based on the Soviet R2 missile, itself a derivative of the German V-2 rocket.

in 1930s America, he and his friends were interested in social issues, reading works of left-wing thinkers including articles by Stalin and Lenin, and debating issues of social justice.

In 1950, as Qian was preparing to go back to China to visit his parents, he was arrested by the FBI, largely for his "complicity" in these early student gatherings. He was stripped of his security clearance and was held under house arrest for five years, and then deported to China. There he would serve as the leader of China's missile and nascent space program, and be the space program's strongest proponent. After Mao's visit to the Soviet Union in 1957, Qian went to Moscow to consolidate Soviet help on the missile program. After months of negotiations, the Soviets gave two R2 missiles to China.

But China might have started a missile program, even before Qian returned to his homeland.

In 1946, while waiting for an invitation to come to the United States to join his fellow Peenemünde rocket

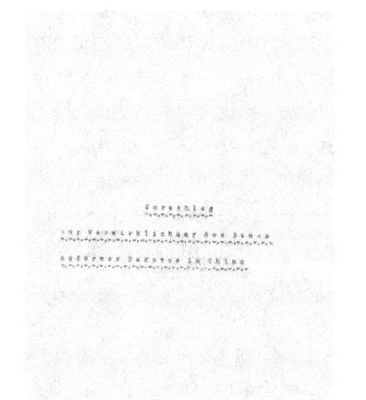

In 1946, while waiting to come to the United States, German visionary Krafft Ehricke developed a proposal for Chinese officials to create a rocket program in China. He proposed that unemployed German rocket experts go to China to create the cadre and manufacturing capability for the future.

The Table of Contents of Krafft Ehricke's China proposal.

team members, space visionary Krafft Ehricke, proposed to Republic of China military representatives in occupied Germany, that unemployed German rocket experts go to China, and help create a rocket program.[1] China would have advanced quickly in developing space technology, had they accepted that proposal.

But as it turned out, the conditions Qian Xuesen found when he returned to China, were rather disheartening for starting a program so advanced as space and rocketry. "We had no research team personnel and metalworking shops." Qian wrote. "At that time my thoughts completely changed, from optimism to pessimism. I really felt that in scientific research it would be difficult to progress even an inch, and I was worried to death about it. I didn't know how to struggle in a difficult environment... how to start from scratch." Nevertheless, by 1958 Qian Xuesen had developed a program with the code name "581" for China to launch a satellite. When adopted, the mission was widely acclaimed and "Launch a satellite" became a national slogan. Children born throughout the country during that time were often named "Weixing," the Chinese word for satellite.

The initial program was to launch suborbital sounding rockets and eventually a satellite. However, the program was delayed by several factors. The break with the Soviet Union in 1960 led to the departure of the hundreds of the Soviet experts who were working in China. The "Great Leap Forward," which was Mao's disastrous forced-march attempt to jump-start the economy without providing the needed economic underpinnings, was followed soon by the cataclysmic "Cultural Revolution," where thousands of leading scientists were rounded up, sent off to the countryside, or even killed. Only a core of the defense-related programs, including rocketry, were somewhat immune from the devastation wreaked by the youthful Red Guards on the intellectual elites of China.

A Halting Beginning

Nevertheless, in February 1960, China succeeded in launching its first indigenously produced liquid-fueled rocket, reaching an altitude of 8 kilometers. In 1964, China launched its first medium-range ballistic missile. In 1962, after the flight of Yuri Gagarin, Qian Xuesen

Deng Xiaoping became the leader of China not long after the death of Mao in 1976. He was responsible for the policy of "reform and opening up" which began the transformation of China into a major economic power. Deng placed the development of science and technology at the center of China's reforms. This photo was taken in 1979.

wrote a book, *Interplanetary Flight*, which stimulated the thinking of Chinese scientists regarding space flight.

In January 1965, Qian began again to put before the Party Central Committee his program for building a satellite. This led to the establishment of the 651 Design Institute, which would be responsible for the project. The first satellite, "The East Is Red 1," was launched on April 24, 1970.

With the end of the Cultural Revolution and the death of Mao in 1976, Deng Xiaoping began his "reform and opening up" policy, which did indeed open up China to the outside world. For several decades, China became the low-wage manufacturing center of the world. But it was not Deng's intention that this would always be the case.

One of the first measures he took was to bring back the exiled professors to the universities, and again open up the universities to all eligible students. He also revived the Chinese Academy of Sciences. But Deng's goal was to resolve many of the economic problems

---

1. See, "A 1946 Proposal for a Chinese Rocket Program," Marsha Freeman, in *History of Rocketry and Astronautics,* 2015, Univelt, for the American Astronautical Society.

facing China after a period of great devastation. While a primitive astronautics program had been initiated in the 1960s, it was canceled by Mao in 1971, for political reasons. While Deng was keen on enhancing China's capabilities in launching satellites, manned space flight was not yet on the agenda, in spite of urgings by Qian Xuesen.

In January 1977 and again in March 1978, Qian sent letters to Chen Xin, the director of the CSTND (Commission for Science, Technology and Industry for National Defense), who had been involved in medical science and in the original astronaut training program, asking for his support for a crash program to get a person into space by 1985, but apparently he was not heeded.

This all changed with the 1983 announcement by President Ronald Reagan, who, under the influence of economist and Presidential candidate Lyndon LaRouche, launched the Strategic Defense Initiative, with its promise of new technological break-throughs. It was clear to some of the key scientists involved in the Chinese satellite program that the U.S. commitment had changed things entirely, and this provoked a major debate at the highest levels in China.

Some Chinese scientists, as related by Gong Xiaohua,[2] argued that missile defense "is not just a military program but a far-reaching political striving to preserve American superiority." In fact, this was an untruth which was being spread deliberately against LaRouche's SDI. In reality, LaRouche and Reagan had always agreed that SDI technologies should be shared with the Soviets, and used worldwide, especially for the industrialization of developing countries. Other Chinese scientists argued that the real objective was "to

China National Space Administration

Each of China's manned Shenzhou missions has advanced China's steps toward a permanent manned presence in space. On the Shenzhou-9 mission in 2008, the first extravehicular activity ("space walk") was conducted. This capability will be needed to assemble the planned space station.

push forward new advanced technologies and national economic development," which was precisely LaRouche's idea for the program, if it is interpreted to mean development of *all* nations.

Some Chinese scientists argued that this required China to rapidly upgrade its own technological level, while others wanted to build up the economic base gradually and not launch any new major technological projects, including human space flight, until they had improved China's economic performance.

Those pushing for a major science-driver program won out, and in March 1986, Chinese planners finalized their plan for research and development, Plan 863. A second dispute arose when the planners presented their proposal to Deng Xiaoping. Would the research be targeted solely to defense needs, or would it be geared to the civilian economy? Deng called for a dual-technology approach. Plan 863 designated seven areas which would be the priorities for development: life sciences, information, energy, defense, automation, new materials, and aerospace.

In February 1987, a special committee was established to develop a detailed plan for the space sector, organized around the operation of a space station in low-Earth orbit, which could be used for the long-term conduct of human scientific experiments. Human space flight was again on the agenda. All told, the 863 Program of scientific research resulted in 2,000 domestic and international patents, and the emergence of an indigenous Chinese IT sector that is today a world leader. In 1997 China issued a new Research program, Plan 973, and in 2013, a further National Key Research and Development Plan was propagated, which incorporated the work of the earlier plans in a more comprehensive structure.

China Puts Men Into Space

The early 1990s brought dramatic changes. The new economic direction of the Chinese leadership, combined with the collapse of the Soviet Union, created

---

2. ``The Inside Story of China's Space Policy Making, 2005," page 263, (in Chinese); quoted in, *A Place for One Man's Mat: China's Space Program, 1956-2003,* by Gregory Kulacki and Jeffrey G. Lewis, 2009, American Academy of Arts & Sciences.

new possibilities for an accelerated and far-reaching Chinese space program

In 1992, Chinese space scientists formulated a development program with the aim of launching a Chinese astronaut into Earth orbit. This was not conceived as a single event, to make a statement or impress either the Chinese people or the world. Rather, just as it was in the eyes of President Kennedy, the German space pioneers, and the leaders of the U.S. space program, the early manned missions would be the first steps to take mankind beyond the Earth, to create a space-faring civilization.

At the same time, many restrictions that had been placed upon the leaders of the former Soviet Union's space program, were gone, and they were now in a position to be able to share their science and technology with the rest of the world. In 1992, Russia created a civilian space agency, and with it the opportunity for international collaboration. For the United States, this made possible the Shuttle/Mir program of mutually-beneficial joint manned orbital missions. For China, it opened the door to gain access, especially in the manned-space field, to Russia's preeminent technology. The first Chinese astronauts were trained in Russia, and the sharing of some of the technology from Russia's Soyuz manned capsule aided the development of China's Shenzhou manned spacecraft.

On the morning of Oct. 14, 2003, a 38-year-old military pilot, Yang Liwei, became the first Chinese astronaut to orbit the Earth. China became only the third nation in the world, after Russia and the United States, to launch a man into space. The decision had been made in 1992 to embark on a manned space program, and since 1998, fourteen Chinese astronauts had been training for the mission.

In fact, China had considered carrying out a manned space program as early as 1967, during the heat of the United States-Soviet space race, but it remained only as a draft program, *Aerospace China* reported in 2003.

Although Yang's mission came decades after Yuri Gagarin's, it was not a simple copy of that world-historic feat. Following China's philosophy of having each

Theo Pirard

At the Naples, Italy International Astronautical Congress in 2012, the authors had the opportunity to meet Liu Yang, the first female Chinese astronaut, who flew on the Shenzhou-9 mission, earlier that year.

space mission break new ground, Yang's Shenzhou-5 spacecraft may have looked like a Russian Soyuz,—but unlike Gagarin's craft, Yang was able to maneuver the Shenzhou, changing its orbit. This would be needed in later missions, in order to rendezvous and dock with other spacecraft.

The mission also included an orbital module, which stayed in space after Yang returned to Earth, and carried out microgravity experiments. In fact, the Shenzhou was nearly twice the mass of the original Soyuz, and was even larger than the vehicles that carry crew to the International Space Station. That first flight was designed in preparation for the much more complex missions to come.

World space experts claimed to be caught by surprise at Yang's flight. But, in the year 2000, the Office of the State Council of China had released, for the first time in English, an eight-page white paper, titled, "China's Space Activities." It was written by Luan Enjie, the head of CNSA (China National Space Administration) from 1998-2006. The paper outlined the goals for the following 20 years. Included were manned space flights, as well as a pre-study of outer-space exploration of the Moon.

The year following Yang's mission, Chinese space officials laid out the step-by-step plan for China's manned space program: multiple-crew missions, extravehicular (space walk) activities, the rendezvous and docking of two space vehicles, the operation of scientific experiments in microgravity, and a man-tended science laboratory,— all to culminate in a space station that can be operated long-term. This is exactly the plan China has been executing.

China has developed the launch, life support, and full array of technologies needed for its manned space program. Shenzhou missions have carried up to three crew members, and have docked with the unmanned Tiangong-1 module both manually and automatically. Astronauts have performed space walks, carried out scientific experiments, all to prepare for the assembly and operation of lengthy stays on its future space station. And to engage everyone, and particularly the young, in this national science-driven exploration, during the 2013 Shenzhou-10 mission, China's second female crew member, Wang Yaping, taught physics lessons to 60 million Chinese students from Earth orbit.

The next step in China's manned space program will be the mid-September launch of the Tiangong-2 module, seen here being completed. A two-man crew will carry out scientific experiments in the small lab for 30 days.

Later this month, China will launch the Tiangong-2 orbital module. Although the same size as the first, the crew will remain in orbit for 30 days, doubling the stay of the previous Tiangong-1 mission. In order to carry the supplies needed for the extended stay, only two crew members, rather than three, will be on the Shenzhou-11 spacecraft that will deliver them to the module, before the end of this year. After the Shenzhou-11 crew has completed their mission, a new unmanned cargo ship, named Tianzhou, similar in function to the Russian Progress cargo ships, will carry out tests with Tiangong-2, including the refueling of the module in orbit.

In 2018, China plans to launch the first component for its space station, which should be fully operational by 2022. The long-range goal is to use the station to prepare for the manned missions into deep space that will follow in the future. The biomedical effects of microgravity and the radiation environment of deep space, the long-lived reliability of space hardware, the psy-

chological impact of a confined habitat, and remote operations, will be tested on the space station in near-by Earth orbit, before Chinese space travelers head for the Moon.

In October 2013, Chinese officials used the occasion of the 64th International Astronautical Congress in Beijing, to invite all other space-faring nations to participate in China's future space station. Astronaut Yang Liwei extended an invitation to foreign space agencies to train crew members for flights on Shenzhou spacecraft to the station. The European Space Agency, its director reported, is already having its astronauts learn Chinese.

The station will include three Chinese laboratory modules, but docking ports will be installed that can accommodate laboratories contributed by other nations.

Deep-Space Exploration

A decade before China's manned space program had achieved its first success in 2003, scientists had been making public their intention to explore the Moon. The most vocal promoter of lunar exploration has been Ouyang Ziyuan.

In a video presentation about Ouyang's life, which aired in 2008, China Central Television (CCTV) relates that his interest in the Moon began in childhood, when

Chinese Academy of Sciences

The father, and chief scientist, of China's lunar program, who created the field of cosmochemistry in China, is Ouyang Ziyuan. Here, he is addressing students in 2010, in his passionate drive to create the next generation of scientists.

he heard the legend of the Chinese princess, Chang'e, and her flight to the Moon. Later, as a geologist, space intrigued him when he studied the impacts of meteorites which had visited Earth from outer space.

His scientific interest turned to the Moon, when, under President Nixon's post-Apollo "Goodwill Rocks" diplomatic initiative, in 1978, China was one of 135 nations to receive a rock from the U.S that Apollo astronauts had brought back from the Moon. This one-half gram lunar sample from our nearest heavenly body was examined by Chinese scientists, and excited Ouyang's imagination, posing more questions about the origin of the Moon than had even been considered before. He originated the study of cosmochemistry in China to enable more challenging studies of the Moon.

In a 2013 interview, Ouyang recalls that in 1992, China's government approved a manned space program, and the following year, the scientists submitted a proposal for the first lunar mission. Three years later, the Academy of Sciences agreed to study the program, and finally, in 1998, the three-phase lunar plan was approved by the Academy. In 2004, the Chang'e series of missions was appproved by the federal government, with Ouyang as the chief scientist.

During the decade that the lunar exploration program was under consideration, Ouyang decided that public education and support would encourage a positive decision by the government. He embarked upon a series of popular science lectures about the Moon, which he has continued to the present day. He has focused on educational institutions, in order to recruit the next generation of scientists and engineers. He believes it is the responsibility of the scientist to create a knowledge and love of science in the population at large.

As far back as 2006, before the first lunar Chang'e-1 mission, Ouyang has been discussing the importance of utilizing lunar resources, singling out the isotope helium-3, rare on Earth, as a fuel for fusion. "Currently nuclear fusion technology is not mature," he explained, "but once it is commercialized, fuel supply will become a problem." "Each year, three Space Shuttle missions could bring back enough fuel for all human beings across the world," he said. In China's three-phase lunar program, the "third target" is to improve our understanding of helium-3 reserves.

In early 2003, Ouyang stated that China is expected to complete its first exploration of the Moon in 2010.

The fruit of Ouyang's decade-long planning of lunar missions is the succession of groundbreaking Chang'e missions to the Moon. Here, the diminutive Chang'e-3 rover, Yutu, which landed on the Moon at the end of 2013, sits amidst the stark lunar landscape. It carried out the first radar investigations of the subsurface of the Moon.

University of Wisconsin, Fusion Technology Center

China plans to not only carry out experiments in order to answer some of the most challenging questions about the Moon, but also to exploit its resources, such as helium-3 as a fuel for fusion energy, which could power the Earth.

Following that, it will establish a base on the Moon. A few months later, he explained that the first in a series of China's robot lunar missions, under its multi-phase China Lunar Exploration Project (CLEP), would be a satellite to orbit the Moon. It would be named Chang'e, after a mythical Chinese princess who flies to the Moon with her pet rabbit, Yutu.

In the second phase, China would place lunar landers on the surface, with remote-controlled rovers,—which it has accomplished. In the third phase, a spacecraft would land, collect samples, and return them to the Earth. This is now scheduled for 2017. Earth's nearest neighbor probably holds the key to humanity's future subsistence and development, says Ouyang. Lunar exploration he said, should be carried out through international cooperation.

China's National Space Administration head, Luan Enjie, speaking at an aerospace conference that year, explained: "The Moon contains various special resources for humanity to develop and use, notably, helium-3. It is a clean, efficient, safe, and cheap new type of nuclear fusion fuel for mankind's future long-term use, and it will help change the energy-resource structure of human society." A news release by *Xinhua News Agency* about Luan's announcement, reported that, "On the Moon, there are between 300,000 and 500,000 tons of Helium-3 reserves. In fusion reactors, it would be capable of sustaining the Earth's electricity [production] for 7,000 years." The mining of helium-3 is a centerpiece of China's goals in lunar exploration.

In 2006, China hosted the eighth conference of the prestigious International Lunar Exploration Working Group, which gathers together the top lunar scientists and mission planners from around the globe. The Beijing Declaration released at that conference committed all space-faring nations to coordinate the operation and scientific results from the array of lunar missions that were being planned, in addition to China, by the United States, Russia, Europe, India, and Japan.

China has carefully followed the progression of lunar missions that was enumerated in its original plan. Chang'e-1, launched in 2007, explored the Moon from lunar orbit. Its scientific instruments analyzed minerals on the surface of the Moon. The Chang'e-2 mission, in 2010, did more detailed mapping, and, after completing its lunar mission, was deployed to a further distance in deep space.

The Chang'e-3 mission captured the imagination of the entire world in 2013, when the lander deployed the 300-pound Yutu (Jade Rabbit) rover on the surface, the first to traverse the Moon since the 1970s. Although Yutu's ability to travel over the lunar surface did not extend past the first cycle of the 14-day lunar night, its ground-penetrating radar and astronomical telescope continued to transmit scientific data, via the lander and orbiter, back to Earth.

Remarking on Jan. 17, 2014 on the significance of China's lunar program, Lyndon LaRouche described the Chang'e-3 landing as "a brilliant enterprise." As do the Chinese scientists, LaRouche stressed that "there is a raw material which has dropped on the Moon as part of the radiation of thermonuclear fusion [from the Sun], essentially that is, of helium-3… which has accumulated on the surface of the Moon, [and] is now the most promising factor in planning the future of the life of the human species." LaRouche added that "if we transmit the benefit of the Moon's accumulation [from the Sun's] thermonuclear fusion, *we are no longer Earthlings*." This formulation echoes that of space visionary Krafft Ehricke, whose extensive plans for the industrial development of the Moon, as the "seventh continent" of the Earth, were based on mankind's "extraterrestrial imperative."

The Chang'e-5T mission, in November 2014, tested technology that will be critical to next year's Chang'e-5 sample return mission, by sending a small capsule from lunar orbit back to Earth. It took this stunning photo of the lunar far side and Earth.

ing the capsule from the surface of the Moon to link up with a craft in lunar orbit, which will head back to Earth, and release the capsule with the samples, to be dropped through the atmosphere.

Other, still more challenging lunar missions are also being planned.

On the Space Frontier

In 2018, China plans to take another bold step in lunar exploration, which, based on its success to date, has been added to the original lunar exploration program. Chang'e-4 will land on the far (non-Earth-facing) side of the Moon, which has never been done by any space agency before. Through photographs taken by orbiters, it is known that the far side of the Moon is significantly different than the face we can see from Earth.

Without a direct line of sight to the Earth, the lander will communicate with Mission Control through an orbiter, which will serve as a relay. The relay satellite is planned to be deployed to the fairly gravitationally-stable L2 point, at a distance of one million miles from the Earth, where it will always have a line of sight to both the lander and the Earth. Even from the earliest fuzzy photographs of the far side of the Moon, sent back from a Russian orbiter in the late 1950s, it could be seen that the hemisphere of the Moon that never faces the Earth, has a different history, topography, and most likely geology and geochemistry, than the Earth-facing near side. Having been sheltered from many of the Earth's effects, it should reveal a more pristine history of the early Solar System.

High-resolution images, most recently delivered by NASA's Lunar Reconnaissance Orbiter, have revealed less evidence of volcanic activity than the near side. There is a higher density of impact craters, including the deepest one on the Moon, located at the south pole. But in addition to what we will learn about the Moon's origin, history, and evolution, the early Earth, and the Solar System,—the far side presents the opportunity to

The success of the Chang'e-3 mission, gave Chinese space planners the confidence to move on to the next step, and re-purpose the back-up spacecraft that had been designated Chang'e-4, were it needed to repeat the landing/roving mission. The new November 2014 mission was designated Chang'e-5T, denoting that it was a test mission for the future mission 5, which will return a lunar sample to Earth. Chang'e-5T successfully swung around the Moon, and carried out a dry run for the future sample return. The mock Return Module successfully plunged through the Earth's atmosphere and was recovered, in a practice run for delivering lunar samples to scientists. The actual Chang'e-5 sample return mission is now scheduled for 2017.

Responding to often-heard complaints from self-appointed U.S. space experts, lunar scientist Paul Spudis told *space.com's* Leonard David after the Chang'e-5T success: "China now has positive practical experience with all of the elements of a human mission to the Moon... And to the brainless twits who might comment that they are only doing something that we have already done, I will simply note that no one at the current incarnation of NASA has done it."

A lunar sample return is a challenging mission which will involve landing a craft, collecting samples, storing them in an hermetically-sealed capsule, launch-

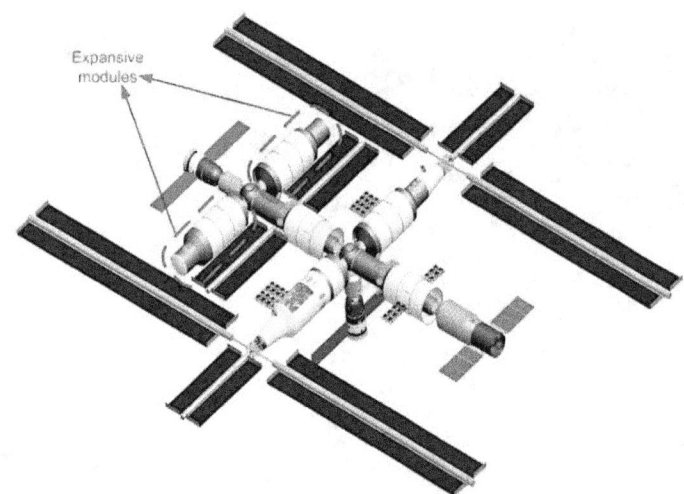

Expansive modules →

As a demonstration of the ability of mankind to live and work in space, and as a stepping stone to the lunar and Mars missions that will follow, China plans to start deploying components for a long-duration space station in 2018, with full operation four years later. In this depiction, the two large cylindrical modules in the center, with the large solar arrays attached, are Chinese experiment modules. The two that are marked "Expansive modules" are docking spaces being offered to other nations who have been invited to send their own laboratories to the station.

look out at the universe in a way we cannot do as well from the Earth, or even from Earth orbit.

The far side of the Moon is shielded from the massive amount of radio signals (noise) coming from our electromagnetically-active Earth civilization. Radio waves, at the very low end of the electromagnetic spectrum, are emitted by galaxies, which will first become revealed by placing radio telescopes on the far side of the Moon. Radio astronomy studies of the Sun and regions of our Solar System will also improve when we can extend the range of frequencies that we can detect.

Beyond the landing on the far side of the Moon, an even more ambitious possible future lunar mission has recently been proposed by scientists, this time to use the Moon to study the Earth.

A group of leading Chinese scientists is conducting a

NASA

No spacecraft has ever landed on the far side of the Moon, which is never seen from the Earth. In this photograph taken by NASA's Lunar Reconnaissance Orbiter, it is easy to recognize that this is not the face we see. Littered with craters and lacking the familiar dark maria, or basaltic "seas," the far side could hold the key to the early evolution of the Earth and the Solar system. Radio astronomy from the electromagnetically quiet far side, will open a new window on the Universe.

feasibility study of building a manned radar station on the Moon, reported the Aug. 21 *South China Morning Post.* The project was launched earlier this year, according to the National Natural Science Foundation of China, with funding for the study of about $2.6 million. Last month, the group met to hold a two-day "brainstorming session."

As noted by the scientists, this project would be a massive undertaking, with many challenges. The lunar-based radar would generate high-intensity beams that could reach the Earth, and the signals received back to the lunar station could provide data on extreme weather conditions, global earthquake activity, the polar ice caps, and other changing features. The advantage of a lunar station over a set of orbiting satellites, explains team leader Prof. Guo Huadong, is that it would provide a wider view than those from the specific locations of orbital satellites. In addition, the Moon is a stable platform, and would have "unlimited durability," in that it could be visited by people, and maintained or repaired.

In order to generate high-intensity radar beams to reach the Earth, a station would need an enormous amount of power, which is one challenge, Guo said in a paper proposing the project three years ago. One reason to have it manned, is that the radar would generate so much data bouncing back from Earth to the lunar station, that it would exceed the long-distance communications bandwidth capability that is now available. On site, astronauts could process the information before sending it back to Earth. At a meeting of the project team in April, the article reports, Chai Yucheng, from the National Science Foundation, said that the government expects a "significant breakthrough" in this proposal by 2020, when the team is to submit its final report.

One broad area of space activity that until recently had

In 2020, China will stretch its astronautical reach further, with its first planned mission to Mars. This model of the lander was recently made public. The mission will include an orbiter, lander, and rover, all on the very first mission to Mars.

not received very much support, is the deployment of scientific satellites, for studies in astronomy, astrophysics, cosmology, biology, and other scientific fields. In 2011, the Chinese leadership, for the first time, authorized a multi-year space science initiative to be carried out during the 12th Five-Year Plan, through 2016. The Strategic Pioneer Research Program in Space Science consists of the development and deployment of up to five space science missions over five years.

As China readied the launch of the first in this series of satellites, in early November last year, Wu Ji, director of the National Space Science Center under the Academy of Sciences, said, "China is the world's second-largest economy, and a major player in space. We should not only be the users of space knowledge, we should also be the creator of space knowledge." Wu added: "China should not only follow others in space exploration; it should set some challenging goals that have never been done by others, such as sending the Chang'e-4 lunar probe to land on the far side of the Moon."

The release of the film "The Martian" in China generated great excitement, as it presented an optimistic view of how man can overcome challenges, and is a call for international cooperation, as it is a Chinese ship that rescues the stranded American astronaut. It is collaboration in Earth-bound great economic projects, and in challenging space missions, the Chinese believe, that will bring mankind into the future.

China's first space observatory, and the first science satellite in the series, the Dark Matter Particle Explorer (DAMPE) was launched last December, and will observe the direction, energy, and electrical charge of high-energy particles in search of dark matter, chief scientist Chang Jin explained. It is described as encompassing the widest spectrum of highest-energy resolution of any dark-matter probe. DAMPE is designed to operate for three years, and will also study the origin of cosmic rays and observe high-energy gamma rays.

The second in the space science series was the launch in April of the Shijian-10. Its capsule, which contained 20 scientific experiments, was returned to Earth for examination of the effects of microgravity.

The ground-breaking Quantum Science Satellite, the third in the series, was just launched on Aug. 16 to test an experimental quantum communications satellite. The Hard X-ray Modulation Telescope, for astronomical studies, is slated for launch this year.

As China explores the Moon, deploys scientific observatories, exploits extraterrestrial resources, such as helium-3, and creates the basis for ambitious manned missions, it has recently also approved its first robotic mission to Mars.

In mid-August, China's space officials released new artists' drawings, a model, and more details about the Mars mission they plan to launch in 2020. Andrew Jones, China space writer for *gb-times* reported on Aug. 23, that in a press conference in Beijing, the chief architect of the mission, Zhang Rongqiao, described it as "complex and ambitious," which is, in fact, an apt description of all of China's deep space missions. This will be China's first mission to Mars, and rather than follow the path of other countries, which carried out a succession of increasingly-complex Mars projects starting with an orbiter, China plans to deploy an orbiter, a lander, and a rover, all on the first mission.

The purpose and scientific goals of the mission are very broad: to use a suite of instruments to study the Martian topography, soil, atmosphere, and water ice. The rover will have a ground-penetrating radar, similar to that on the lunar rover Yutu, and will examine the internal structure of the planet. Lunar mission scientist Ye Peijian reports that the Mars rover is being developed by the same team that carried out the Chang'e-3 lunar lander/Yutu rover mission. Jones reports that Zhang said that this ambitious mission will also be a demonstration of the technology needed for a Mars sample-return mission around 2030.

During the favorable 2020 launch opportunity to Mars, missions will be launched by the United States, and by Russia for Europe. Japan will launch a small craft for the UAE. NASA and ESA missions that are now in development, aim to gather samples on Mars, as the first step to eventually returning the rocks and soil to Earth in the future. As China has the same goal, this is exploration that is ripe for international cooperation.

China's goals for its space exploration programs are no less, and no different fundamentally, than those of other nations. What is unique about China's space program, however, is the way it is seen by the country's political, as well as scientific, leadership. China's space programs are being pursued as a leading feature of a multi-decade thrust into the future, which will be shaped by the pace of advancements in science and technology.

While other efforts in human space exploration have languished in the wake of the world financial crisis and ensuing social chaos in many parts of the world, China is pointing the way forward in the "new frontier" of space. Chinese efforts have already generated great enthusiasm worldwide for manned space exploration. The world is waiting for the United States, the first nation to put a man on the Moon, to grasp the supreme importance of cooperating with China and other nations, in expanding the realm of human activity into the galaxy that is our common home.

Philippines Prepares To Go Nuclear As Part of New World Paradigm

by Michael Billington

Sept. 3 (EIRNS)—The Philippines has been the economic basket case of Southeast Asia ever since the United States, under Secretary of State George Shultz and Assistant Secretary Paul Wolfowitz orchestrated a coup against its nationalist leader, President Ferdinand Marcos, in 1986, one of the first "color revolutions" run by the Project Democracy team in Washington. Before that criminal act, the Philippines was the envy of Southeast Asia, and even of South Korea, as the leader in industrialization, food self-sufficiency, and economic development generally.

Now, finally, after 30 years, the Philippine people have thrown out the crew of subservient leaders who answered only to Washington and Wall Street, and have begun to clean out the filth and relieve the suffering left behind—drugs, terrorism, hunger and poverty—under the newly elected President Rodrigo Duterte, who took office on June 30.

The most blatant and disgusting symbol of the coup against the Philippine people and nation in 1986 was the immediate shutting down of the Bataan Nuclear Power Plant by Cory Aquino upon her installation as President, on orders from Washington. The plant, launched by Marcos in 1974 and built by Westinghouse, was complete and ready to be turned on, but never produced a watt of electricity. Aquino nonetheless promised Wall Street that the country would pay every peso

Malacañang Photo Bureau

Then President-elect Rodrigo Roa Duterte, on June 30, 2016.

of the cost of the plant, which it did, even as the Philippines economy and standard of living plummeted to its current disastrous state.

However, between August 30 and September 1 of this year, the International Atomic Energy Agency (IAEA) sponsored a conference in Manila on "Prospects for Nuclear Power in the Asia-Pacific." The new Duterte Government took full advantage of the IAEA forum as the opportunity to both declare its intent to re-open the Bataan Nuclear Plant and to launch a mass education campaign to counter the lies and fearmongering of the anti-nuclear mafia controlled by the West.

Energy Secretary Alfonso Cusi told the press that the conference had provided him and others with a "virtual crash course on the entire chain of launching a nuclear program and the importance of public information." He said that he and others had visited the Bataan Nuclear Power Plant (BNPP) Thursday morning. "The timing of this summit is perfect," Cusi said. "As a coincidence we had a hearing also in the Senate. We discussed also nuclear power plants, and today we inspected the BNPP and there are a lot of discussions," he said.

Butch Valdes, the head of the Philippines LaRouche Society, had organized a tour of the Bataan plant for politicians, engineers, and others in 2008, which sparked the growing interest in reversing the disastrous decision to mothball the plant. Valdes has since been

PLS

Right to left: Philippines LaRouche Society (PLS) leader Ver Archivido, head of the PLS Butch Valdes, and Cathy Cruz at the IAEA conference in Manila.

the leading spokesman for restoring the Bataan plant as the necessary spark for restoring economic growth, and was invited to address the IAEA conference, to speak on the role of the public in countering the anti-nuclear, anti-science lies, and on using the issue of nuclear power to mobilize the creativity of the people to create a future of human dignity for all. His powerful speech is included in this issue.

Duterte vs. Obama's War and Poverty Agenda

The Duterte government's courageous stand is not only transforming the Philippines, but has dramatically changed the entire dynamic of Southeast Asia and Asia generally. His policies have sent the Obama government and the Wall Street controlled NGOs into hysterics, but he has increasingly won the hearts and minds of a grateful nation, while joining proudly with the Chinese-led process of cooperation for development centered on the New Silk Road process. Some crucial points:

• Upon his inauguration, Duterte immediately set in motion the process of reconciliation with China, essentially ignoring the imperial court set up in the Hague which ruled in an illegal arbitration that China has no historic claims in the South China Sea. Obama and his neocon allies were ready to act immediately after the decision to provoke a military confrontation with China, but Duterte's move quashed that effort. Duterte said openly and clearly that the Philippines needs infrastructure and industrial development above all, which, he said, is only available from the China-centered new paradigm.

• Duterte's Defense Secretary, Gen. (ret.) Delfin Lorenzana, told the press that the Philippine defense budget would no longer waste money on ships and planes designed to confront China in the South China Sea, since "there will be no war." Instead the budget will shift to helicopters, coast guard vessels, night vision equipment, and other material needed to fight the terrorist scourge and the interrelated drug crisis across the country.

• Duterte declared a war on drugs, and is carrying it out in earnest, not in name only. While the West focusses on the hundreds of people who have been killed in the newly escalated war, they ignore the fact that 600,000 people have turned themselves in, and that the President has publicly named many elected officials and several leading generals in the police and the military who were protecting the drug traffickers. He has sworn to wipe out the drug scourge within six months.

• Duterte has also sworn to wipe out the Abu Sayyaf terrorist kidnapping gang, which has sworn allegiance to ISIS. The Saudi-linked jihadist gang has beheaded their kidnap victims, both Filipino and foreign, when the demanded ransoms were not paid. The battles have already begun in the southern islands of Sulu Province, and Duterte has deployed 2,500 extra troops to the battle. At the same time, he and the leaders of the long-festering communist insurgency have agreed to a cease fire and are working towards a peace agreement and integration of the insurgents into civil society. Crucial to this has been Duterte's pledge to address the needs of the impoverished and hungry masses. He is also working towards a peaceful resolution with the Islamic separatist groups in Mindanao, but not the terrorists.

• Although Duterte had a productive meeting with U.S. Secretary of State John Kerry, who encouraged the new President to proceed with his plans to meet with the Chinese to find bilateral solutions to the South China Sea conflict, Duterte publicly denounced U.S. Ambassador to the Philippines Philip Goldberg, who throughout the election campaign openly attacked Duterte, illegally attempting to infuence the election. Also, when Goldberg confronted Duterte to live up to the country's "pledge" at the Paris Global Warming conference, Duterte rejected it outright, saying that his country needed industrial development, and refused to limit carbon emissions which would undermine that urgent necessity. Told that the Philippines must live up to its signature on the Paris agreement, he responded that "that was not my signature." Goldberg had been thrown out of Bolivia in 2008 when, as U.S. Ambassador, he openly backed a separatist movement there.

• Duterte has also declared that he will allow the Marcos family to bury the late President Ferdinand Marcos in the Hero's Cemetery in Manila, established after World War II for Filipino military personnel from privates to generals who served during World War II

(over 33,000), and later designated a National Pantheon, "to perpetuate the memory of all the Presidents of the Philippines, national heroes and patriots for the inspiration and emulation of this generation and of generations still unborn." The presidents subservient to Washington since the coup against Marcos have refused to allow his burial in the Hero's Cemetery. This action will further restore the legacy of Marcos as one of the great leaders of post-war Asia, whose removal led (as intended) to the destruction of the nation economically and morally.

'I like Putin Better—We're Alike'

When asked by the press on Aug. 30 whether he would respond to President Obama at their planned meeting at the ASEAN Summit in Laos on Sept. 6, after Obama said he would confront Duterte over human rights and the rule of law, Duterte said it depended on whether or not Obama were willing to listen first: "They must understand the problem first before we talk about human rights. I would insist, 'Listen to me. This is what the problem is.' Then we can talk. No problem."

Asked about his planned meeting with Vladimir Putin, Duterte said: "I like Putin better. We're alike."

Why the Philippines Will Go Nuclear

Address of Antonio "Butch" Valdes to the International Atomic Energy Agency (IAEA) Conference on the Prospects for Nuclear Power in the Asia-Pacific Region, Manila, Aug. 30-Sept. 1, 2016. Valdes was introduced by Dr. Kenneth Peddicord, Director of the Nuclear Power Institute (NPI) of Texas and a professor of nuclear engineering at Texas A&M University.

Dr. Peddicord: I'm pleased to welcome to the podium a gentleman I sat next to yesterday, and really enjoyed the conversations with him, Antonio "Butch" Valdes, who is with an NGO, the Save the Nation Movement, here in the Philippines. He has worked as a columnist at the *Business World*, a publisher and columnist at the *News Daily*, the *Independent*, and the *Observer*, as a radio commentator, the founding president of the Chamber of Filipino Entrepreneurs, the chairman of the Philippines LaRouche Society, and he's served as Undersecretary of the Department of Education, Culture and Sports. ... He's a former president of the De La Salle University Alumni Association, Asian History of

Management Alumni Association, and the Association of Certified Public Accountants in Public Practice.

He holds a degree in Liberal Arts in Commerce, with a major in political science and accounting from De La Salle University and a master's degree in management from the Asian Institute of Management. Please join me in welcoming Butch Valdes to the podium.

Antonio "Butch" Valdes: Thank you very much. There were a few lines there that I was not familiar with, but thank you anyway. [laughter]

Let me be the initiator of a change of pace. But from the outset, I'd like to, on behalf of my fellow Filipinos here, I'd like to thank the IAEA, and of course, the Department of Energy, for creating this particular conference, a conference which could not have been timed in a more appropriate period, and especially here in our country.

I am one of those who have been pushing for nuclear energy for quite some time now, over 15 years as a matter of fact, but that was not because I knew a lot about nuclear energy, at the time, but more because I had looked into it—as a layman, as a businessman—not

PLS

Presentation by head of the PLS, Butch Valdes, at the IAEA conference in Manila, Aug. 29, 2016.

as a scientist—as an economist, a businessman, and a professional.

I, together with many other Filipinos, was asking myself, what has happened to our country, and where is it going? There is a saying in the Philippines, in our language, so I'll try to paraphrase it: When you don't know where you come from, you don't know where you are, you will not know where you are going. The Filipinos here would understand what I mean. So, in order to be able to do this, you had to dig up a little in the past, and see what has happened. I was a bit unclear about certain periods, but after knowing a little bit about those periods, I began to realize that there was a process, a process that brought us to this particular situation.

As far as nuclear power is concerned, I have to start in the period where the whole world was shocked in 1945, when the atomic bomb was exploded—the only time that a nuclear bomb was ever exploded in the whole history of mankind, and it created such an impression on the rest of the world—including of course my parents; I was not yet alive during that time—but this kind of shock and awe that was created at that time, led to a kind of mindset, most especially, in my experience here in our country.

Eisenhower's Pledge to the World

So we realized that the United States, after Harry Truman dropped that bomb,— that the next President realized that he had to correct a certain image and an understanding of what nuclear energy really was. And I am happy that the IFNEC [International Framework for Nuclear Cooperation] and the IAEA promote Atoms for Peace, because the very first organization that we had put together in pushing for nuclear energy was called the Atoms for Peace Movement. And it was in line with the program that President Eisenhower had initiated in the United States to present to the whole world. He called it the Atoms for Peace program.

And the whole objective was a success here. Let me read it together with you: "To the making of these fateful decisions, the United States pledges before you—and therefore before the world—its determination to help solve the fearful atomic dilemma—to devote its entire heart and mind to find the way by which the miraculous inventiveness of man shall not be dedicated to his death, but consecrated to his life."[1]

---

1. An extract from President Dwight D. Eisenhower's address to the UN General Assembly, Dec. 8, 1953.

For some, of course, from the United States, this might be ordinary, but for us, in the rest of the world, it was inspiring. And it inspired us so much that we, I'm sure, communicated with the government of the United States and we became the first recipient of this particular Atoms for Peace program. Soon after, we were granted the resources and the technical help to put up a reactor, a 2 megawatt reactor, and to start the Philippine Atomic Energy Commission, which is the precursor of what we now know as the PNRI, the Philippine Nuclear Research Institute.

During this time, which was in the 1950s, there were attempts, of course, and the continuous study of what nuclear energy could do, for peaceful means, in terms of our economy, in terms of our agricultural production, and the possibility of industrialization. But at that time, these benefits had already been shown to us, but because, I suppose, because of the low cost of oil at the time, the effort to go into nuclear was not as urgent as later on, and this became the decision of government. It was not as urgent because, well, there were politics involved, but the other thing was that oil was just that cheap.

Nixon Pulls the Plug

But some time in 1971, the economic order changed. During this period between 1946 and 1971, the whole world was being run by a certain economic order that came out of the Bretton Woods agreement; that Bretton Woods agreement basically meant that there will be fixed exchange rates, which means there would be no fluctuation on currency exchanges; no fluctuations, it was fixed. And the IMF was the one that was supposed to be moderating this. And aside from that, of course, usury was considered to be a crime, and it was a crime during this particular period. People who were charging excessive interest rates were charged because of the anti-usury law.

This was all the way up to 1971. Just imagine if the exchange rates were fixed. People could, at that time, start looking for long-term investments, because if the exchange rates were fixed, the interest rates do not fluctuate. And if the interest rates do not fluctuate, the cost of money stays stable, and you as an investor would be able to project yourself, 20, 30 years on. And that's exactly what was happening.

So, if that is the case, a lot of money, resources, could go into the physical economy, infrastructure.

However, in 1971, initiated also by the United States, President Nixon pulls the plug and says, the world will be going to a different economic order, and we were going into a floating exchange rate. Now, these floating exchange rates allowed money to be a commodity, because, since it was varying in relationship with other currencies, it became an object of investment. That's why it became more difficult, right at that time, to start investing in infrastructure, somethings that you will need over long-term gestation periods.

Now this condition made it difficult for us, because the IMF took the lead for the financial institutions to start imposing certain rules. I still remember the time when they told us—at that time the President was President Marcos—

PLS

Right to left: PLS head Butch Valdez, DOE Secretary Alfonso Cusi, and Dr. Carlito R. Aleta, former Director of the Philippine Nuclear Energy Institute, at the IAEA conference in Manila, Aug. 29, 2016.

they told us that we needed to devalue our currency vis-à-vis the U.S. dollar, and that they considered our currency to be overvalued—it was at that time more or less about 4 pesos to $1—and that we needed to divide it immediately to 8 pesos to $1.

You can just imagine the kind of shock that this was going to do to us. Under the threat that we will not be granted the resources by the banking sector to be able to import our oil, if we did not devalue, we devalued, not exactly to 8, but pretty close to 8. And subsequent devaluations then happened: Just imagine, if we needed only 4 pesos to pay $1 debt, in a very short period of time, if you bring it all the way up to 1986, we would need 28 pesos to pay $1, and that was going to be borne by the population. But that is the system, and we still went, nevertheless.

A Coup to Stop Industrialization

Because of this pressure that was extended to us, Mr. Marcos decided in 1974, to go into an energy development program—a program which was going to be based on three baseload activities. One was geothermal, another was hydroelectric, and a third was nuclear. Of course, we went into all of this, including nuclear, but the nuclear portion took a little bit more time.

As part of this nuclear energy development program, he pushed what we called an 11-point industrialization program. This whole industrialization program was going alongside an energy development program, a program which he expected to make the country energy self-sufficient by 1990. This did not happen.

Sometime in 1986 we had a revolution. We couldn't start our nuclear power plant, for one reason or another. In 1985, we were ready to fire it, but this was stopped, because, according to U.S. Ambassador Bosworth at the time, they wanted to take a look at the condition of the plant. There were no questions about the condition of the plant. They said that the gates and the perimeter needed more security against terrorists and the hospitals that were in the vicinity—a 30-mile vicinity—were not Class A hospitals, they were Class B and C hospitals; they did not count the Class A hospital that was only about 10 kilometers away from the nuclear power plant, that is, in the Subic Bay [i.e., in the U.S. military base—ed.]. This was the situation.

By the time we hit 1986, revolution—and the coming administration decided to mothball what was an otherwise ready-to-operate nuclear power plant. And of course—for some people this might be obvious, but others might not see through what I'm saying—there were definite plans, as far as I'm concerned, for us not to go industrial, and to stop us from this whole energy development program would have stopped us, as earlier said, yesterday by Congressman Mark Cojuangco.

Service Economies Don't Need Scientists

The rest of Southeast Asia also did not go nuclear. Why? I'll let you answer that. But you see what had happened. At the same time that this thing was being mothballed, a major economic thrust was being pushed. They called it "globalization." The globalization program was to convert economies which were otherwise *producer economies*, or setting themselves up to be producer economies, into service economies, which meant they were going to make use of our cheap labor, through,— if you know how cheap labor is generated— they continue to devalue your currency vis-à-vis their own. As you get cheaper, you are now given contracts to do the work which they could not do anymore because it's too expensive. So we became precisely *that* kind of economy.

And during that period, we stopped producing scientists. What we produced were nurses, caregivers, culinary arts people, and other areas of service. I am not denigrating them; this is where the education institutions went, because that was where the work was. So this is the situation.

Again, from a standpoint of politics, I will let you answer that. But for us, what we see here and the reason nuclear was very important, we know that man is the only creature that has been able to use fire for its benefit. And using fire for its benefit, it was on that, that the development of man, the whole history of mankind, was based—in the *whole history* of mankind.

We Are Promethean

We refer, of course, very often pedagogically to a guy named Prometheus. Prometheus as you know was the one who brought the beneficial use of fire to mortals, despite what Zeus was saying. And for this he was punished. Our national hero, José Rizal, even sculpted a figure of Prometheus being tied to a rock, to be eaten by vultures, because he has defied Zeus, because he had taught mortals the beneficial use of fire.

Now, the IAEA is doing precisely what Prometheus was doing, but it will not be tied to a rock. And we are going to move very quickly, through the leadership of—of course—yourselves, and it is through you that this kind of thinking that we have, makes us more inspired. Because together you understand what man has to do in order to face up to those interests that are decided, that are determined, to try to prevent man from developing. But as you see, over the last 70 years, despite all of these efforts, the world and humankind is moving forward.

I mentioned earlier the value of fusion energy, and reprocessing. I say this not because I am a scientist, but because I read that man continues, *continues* to study all kinds of solutions for possible problems that we will be facing. Because we had gone through a whole history, where we first discovered the benefit of fire from wood, and as we discovered the technology, we then had what you call the capacity to sustain an even greater population. And every stage of the way, *every* stage, after wood, we discovered coal; after coal, we discovered oil; and after oil we discovered nuclear fission. The next will be nuclear fusion. And probably the next will be something else, like matter-antimatter reactions. But all of this is within our capability, maybe not the present IAEA, but the succeeding one, the succeeding organizations that will go there.

Because after all, if we are to assure ourselves of continued existence, we must use what we've all been given, whether I'm an accountant, an economist, a scientist, an educator, or any ordinary businessman, we have that capability to be creative—imagination. Imagination is cheap, but it yields the highest return on that investment.

Valdes responded to a question regarding the antinuclear power organizations.

Valdes: I found out over the years, so many years, that we've been presented with so much disinformation—I'm sorry, they are not my colleagues, so I don't mind denigrating them.

This is a campaign, a campaign that is being waged, a fear campaign for us to get out of science, for countries like us and people like us not to go into scientific inquiry and not to latch onto scientific truth, and to be affected by other types of campaigns which have different objectives. And that is, I suppose, a reality of humankind. There are those that will not want you to develop because their objective is to control other humans.

On the other hand, it is truth which is the basis of true science. Let me interject, that there are scientists, and there are scientists. There are those that are of course motivated differently. But there is true science. And the fact that the IAEA and the technology which is nuclear technology has been around for 70 years and it is still going strong, still affecting lives positively all over the world, that is a true testament of what scientific truth is. No matter what campaigns are being waged for the moment, they will die off. Because eventually, truth will be the basis. You just have to steady the ship, stay focussed, just steady as it goes—and go for it.

Financial 'Rapists' Win a Battle, Not the War, with Coup Against Brazil's President

by Gretchen Small

Sept. 5—On July 16-18, 2014, President Dilma Rousseff hosted the VI Summit of the BRICS nations—Brazil, Russia, India, China and South Africa—in Fortaleza, Brazil, with the heads of state of all the Union of South American Nations (Unasur), joined by representative heads of state from Mexico, the Caribbean, and Central America. It was at the Fortaleza summit that the agreement was reached to establish the BRICS New Development Bank, and the BRICS emerged as an independent global force, committed, as Rousseff said, to end "any kind of dependency," and to seek, "for ourselves our scientific and technological autonomy," among other goals.

And because of Brazil's role, all of South America was in on it.

Two years and a few weeks later, this past Aug. 31, Dilma Rousseff was impeached by the Senate of Brazil on spurious charges, for crimes which she did not commit. Former Argentine President Cristina Fernández de Kirchner, who played an important role herself at that 2014 summit, immediately named the BRICS, and South America's participation with it, as the strategic target of this "coup."

On Sept. 1, Fernández told Radio 10's Roberto Navarro, host of its *Economía Política* TV program that Brazil, Ecuador, Bolivia, and her own government (before her term ended in December 2015) were being targeted for having adopted a more independent foreign policy, and allying with Russia and China.

Asked by Navarro whether she was saying that the United States was reacting to the foreign policy adopted by Dilma, herself, and others, she responded that "the meeting that Dilma held in Brazil, between Mercosur, Unasur, and the BRICS, did not sit very well with the extra-continental powers" behind the coup against Rousseff.

The coup was "a component of a regional destabilization, coming from domestic and foreign concentrated

Construction work on the Santo Antônio Dam in Rondônia in 2009, with Growth Acceleration Program (PAC) funds. PAC was a major infrastructure program of the Federal government of Brazil.

Marcello Casal JR/ABr

economic sectors," she said. The "superpowers" responsible for carrying it out are orchestrating "a harsh strategy against popular governments and their leaders," an evaluation with which *EIR* Founding Editor Lyndon LaRouche heartily concurred.

The Next Battle Is On

Leaving the presidential Alvorada Palace after the Senate voted to impeach her, President Rousseff made clear that the fight for Brazil is not over, but will escalate:

"The progressive, inclusive, and democratic national project which I represent is being interrupted by a powerful, conservative, and reactionary force.... They intend to capture the institutions of the State to place them at the service of the most radical economic liberalism and social regression....

"Listen well: They think that they have defeated us, but they are mistaken. I know that we are all going to fight. There will be the most unfaltering, untiring, and energetic opposition that a putschist government can bear.... We will return to continue our journey towards a Brazil in which the people are sovereign."

Rousseff's forceful testimony in her own defense during the impeachment trial (see accompanying speech by Dilma), won international public recognition, albeit grudging, that her impeachment had no legitimacy, but was a modern form of coup. Even France's *Le Monde* and Germany's *Der Spiegel* were forced to admit it.

The charge on which she was impeached,—that she ordered supplementary credits to cover budget gaps in alleged violation of a balanced budget law—which had been done by every recent Brazilian government,—was already preposterous. But then, the Brazilian Congress passed Law 31.332/2016 on Sept. 2, which legalized the very budget accounting practice for which Dilma had been impeached two days before!

Even Rio de Janeiro State University law professor Ricardo Lodi, who testified in Rousseff's defense

Agencia Brazil

Children in one of the favelas (slums and shanty towns) in Rio de Janeiro at the time of the World Cup. There is no sanitation or place to play

during the trial, was astonished. He told *Jornal do Brasil* that the new law confirmed what he had said in the Senate: "this procedure was never illegal before and it won't be so later. It was only deemed a crime for approving impeachment. They didn't even have the modesty to cover it up!"

Brazil's Deputy Attorney General Ela Wiecko resigned her post on the eve of the impeachment vote, as a protest against this "coup," and informed *Veja* magazine that "there are many people who think the way I do within the institution."

Playing with Fire

Wall Street's pathetic Brazilian puppet "President" Michel Temer, spent much of his time at the Hangzhou G-20 summit issuing assurances that with Dilma out, Brazil will quickly regain economic and political stability.

This is a fraud. No government, neither Temer's nor any usurper combination, could "stably" impose upon Brazil the level of looting and loss of sovereignty which Wall Street and the British Empire's Obama are demanding. The foreign forces which put Temer in power know this. He is just a throw-away placeholder on the way to the complete takedown of Brazil as a nation.

Wall Street's Brazilian President for the moment, Michel Temer.

Senator Roberto Requião, from the state of Paraná, warned during the impeachment trial that the economic plans of those behind this coup are sowing the seeds of civil war. Like Rousseff in her testimony, he detailed the plans of the financial and geopolitical "vultures and crows" behind the coup, to impose a 20-year freeze on all expenditures and investments for health, sanitation, education, infrastructure, housing, and public security. They will guarantee payment of interest on the debt, and privatize the nation's energy, mineral, agricultural, manufacturing, and technological patrimony.

He asked: "Are you gentlemen and ladies prepared for civil war? No? Then dig your trenches, because conflict will be inevitable. The Brazilian people who have tasted the pleasure of social advancement for some years, will not return submissively to the slave quarters."

Taking On Brazil Itself

Is this a battle between the "left" and the "right," as stupid commentaries insist? The forces currently debating amongst themselves how to save the nation are far broader.

Sen. Requião, who calls himself a socialist, for example, is part of a nationalist "Alliance for Brazil" movement founded in 2015 to join together people and groups of differing political and ideological outlooks who are committed to defending national sovereignty, Brazil's people, and national development. Its members range from the Brazilian Lawyers Association to representatives of the nuclear, oil, engineering, and heavy construction industries, and it overlaps the advanced military-defense industry sector.

These forces understand they are up against the interests of bankers and financiers, unproductive parasites who know nothing and care nothing about the people or nation of Brazil. Rio's heavyweight Engineers' Club, a leading force within the Alliance, issued a statement last June 17, listing initiatives taken by the impeachers which would take down the nation's in-depth productive capabilities, including constitutional amendments to block completion of Brazil's mastery of the full nuclear fuel cycle and privatize the two nuclear plants already operating; privatize the state oil company, Petrobras; turn the pre-salt oil fields over to foreign interests; change the mining code to favor foreign multinationals; and allow unlimited purchases of land by foreigners to use as they please.

The goal is "to relegate us to the condition of raw materials suppliers. It is the return to Colony Brazil," the engineers wrote.

This War Will Be Won Globally

These forces also know that the world has changed, as was most dramatically demonstrated in the G-20 Summit which concluded today in Hangzhou, China. Despite the setbacks in South America, the train that left the station at the Fortaleza summit has not been derailed; it is accelerating. The threat is increasing for the financial "rapists"—as LaRouche dubbed them—who ran the coup in Brazil. South American patriots are turning to that global reality, as they regroup their forces for a counter-attack.

Brazilian veteran journalist Mauro Santayana's biting Aug. 30 column, "Herr Schiemer and the Future of Brazil" is indicative of the spirit developing in Brazil and elsewhere in the region. Responding to the ultimata of the head of Mercedes-Benz in Brazil, Santayana wrote that Schiemer offers Brazil a return to "the old world of the time of the Persian or Roman empire, where colonies or countries had to accommodate their productive systems to foreign economic groups." But, now there is "the new world of China," he went on. The Chinese model is completely different. "Beijing invests directly in everything related to technology [and] improves the living conditions and consumption of the population."

ROUSSEFF'S COUNTERATTACK

'Do Not Expect from Me
The Obsequious Silence of Cowards'

The following are excerpts from the 45-minute speech given on Aug. 29, 2016 by Brazilian President Dilma Rousseff, at her impeachment trial before the Brazilian Senate.

Marcelo Camargo/Agency Brazil

President Roussef defending herself during the impeachment trial in the Senate.

"I was elected with more than 54 million votes. At my inauguration, I assumed the commitment to defend and obey our Constitution, whether in the observation of our laws, the promotion of the general welfare of the Brazilian people, or maintaining the unity, integrity, and independence of Brazil. In exercising the Presidency of the Republic, I faithfully respected the commitment I assumed before the nation and those who elected me. And I am proud of that ...

"I have also heard harsh criticisms of my government, of the errors which were committed and the measures and policies which were not adopted. I welcome those criticisms with humility. Because, like everyone, I have defects and I make mistakes. But disloyalty and cowardice are not among my defects. I do not betray the commitments I assume, the principles I defend, or those who fight at my side. In the fight against the dictatorship, I received on my body the marks of torture. I endured the suffering of jail for years ... But I did not change sides ... I fought for a society where there would not be misery or excluded ones. I fought for a sovereign, more equitable Brazil, where there would be justice. I am also proud of that. Those who believe, fight ...

"Do not expect from me the obsequious silence of cowards. In the past, with arms, and today, with juridi-

cal rhetoric, they again intend to attack democracy and the Rule of Law ...

"I am not fighting for my term of office ... I know that I am about to be judged, once again. And it is because I have an absolutely clear conscience regarding what I did, in the exercise of the Presidency of the Republic, that I come personally into the presence of those who will judge me ... to say, with the serenity of those who have nothing to hide, that I did not commit any crime of responsibility ...

"Today Brazil, the world, and history are watching us and await the outcome of this impeachment process. In Latin America and Brazil's past, whenever the interests of the economic and political elite were hurt at the polls, and there were no legal grounds for a legitimate removal of the government, conspiracies were plotted which led to coups d'etat ...

"Today, once again, finding the interests of the

economic and political elite thwarted and hurt at the polls, we are facing the risk of a rupture of democracy. The dominant political standards in the world reject explicit violence. Now, the rupture of democracy occurs by moral violence and constitutional pretexts to lend the appearance of legitimacy to a government which is taking power without support from the polls. The Constitution is invoked so that the world of appearances hypocritically covers up the world of facts ...

"They are pretext, only pretexts, to overthrow, by a process of impeachment where there is no crime of responsibility, a legitimate government chosen through direct elections and with the participation of 110 million Brazilian men and women. The government of a woman who dared to win two consecutive presidential elections. They are pretexts to justify a coup against the Constitution. A coup which, if it is consummated, will result in the indirect election of a usurping government ...

"What is at stake is respect for the polls, the sovereign will of the Brazilian people, and the Constitution. What is at stake are the conquests of the last 13 years: the advances of the population, of the poorest people and of the middle class, the protection of children; the youth going to universities and technical schools; the improvement of the minimum wage; the doctors caring for the population; the realization of the dream of having your own house. What is at stake is the investment in public works to ensure survival during droughts and semi-arid conditions, and the conclusion of the long awaited and dreamed of project for the integration of the San Francisco river. What is at stake, as well, is Brazil's great discovery, the pre-salt oil deposits. What is at stake is our country's sovereign insertion into the world stage, guided by ethics and the search for common interests. What is at stake is the self-respect of Brazilian men and women ... What is at stake is the future of the country, the opportunity and the hope of always progressing further ...

"They are pretexts, to overthrow, by a process of impeachment, a legitimate government chosen through direct elections and with the participation of 110 million Brazilian men and women ... pretexts to justify a coup against the Constitution. A coup which, if it is consummated, will result in the indirect election of a usurping government ..."

"What is at stake is the future of the country, the opportunity and the hope of always progressing further... The most frightening threat of this impeachment process is the freezing for 20 years of all spending on health, education, sanitation, housing."

"The most frightening threat of this impeachment process without any crime of responsibility, is the freezing for 20 years of all spending on health, education, sanitation, housing. It is preventing for 20 years that more children and youth have access to schools; that for 20 years, people be able to receive better health care; that for 20 years, families be able to dream of having their own house ...

"As is characteristic of the conservative and authoritarian elites, they did not see in the will of the people the legitimizing element of a government. They wanted power, at any price. They did everything to destabilize me and my government ...

"Everyone knows that I did not enrich myself through the exercise of public posts, that I did not embezzle public funds to my personal benefit nor to that of my relatives, and that I do not own accounts or property abroad. I have always acted with absolute probity in public posts that I have held throughout my life ...

"We are one step away from consummating a grave institutional rupture. We are one step away from concretizing a true coup d'etat ...

"Twice I have looked death in the face: when I was tortured for days on end, subjected to cruelty which makes one doubt humanity and the meaning of life itself; and when a serious and very painful illness threatened to shorten my existence. Today, I only fear for the death of democracy, for which many of us, here in this plenary, fought with our best efforts....

"Remember that in a presidential system and under the aegis of our Constitution, a political conviction necessarily requires that a crime of responsibility have happened, committed intentionally, and that it be thoroughly proven. Remember the terrible precedent that this decision may create for other presidents, governors, and mayors. To convict without substantive evidence. To convict an innocent person. I make a final appeal to all the Senators: Do not accept a coup which will only worsen, rather than solve, the Brazilian crisis."

Every Day Counts In Today's Showdown To Save Civilization

That's why you need EIR's **Daily Alert Service**, a strategic overview compiled with the input of Lyndon LaRouche, and delivered to your email 5 days a week.

For example: On Jan. 7, EIR's Daily Alert featured the British hand behind the pattern of global provocations toward war. Of special note is British Intelligence's role in instigating the Saudi Kingdom's attempt to set off a Sunni-Shia war. This religious war has been the intent of British strategy since the Blair-Bush attack on Iraq in 2003.

We also uniquely update you regularly on the progress toward the release of the suppressed 28 pages of the Congressional Inquiry on 9/11, which would expose the Saudi role.

Every edition highlights the reality of the impending financial crash/bail-in policies that would realize the British goal of mass depopulation.

This is intelligence you need to act on, if we are going to survive as a nation and a species. Can you really afford to be without it?

THURSDAY, JANUARY 7, 2016

Volume 2, Number 97

EIR Daily Alert Service

P.O. Box 17390, Washington, DC 20041-0390

- British Crown Pushing War and Genocide in 2016
- Financial Mudslide Goes On; Monetarist Tyranny Gloats over Bail-Ins
- Moody's Downgrades Portugal's Novo Banco
- Puerto Rico's Default: It's Every Vulture for Himself
- Wide Glass-Steagall Debate Set Off Again by Sanders Speech
- MI6 Mouthpiece Evans-Pritchard Touts Persian Gulf Chaos
- North Korea Tests a Miniaturized Hydrogen Bomb
- Uighur Terrorists Found in Indonesia
- Foreign Investors Are Flocking In to China

EDITORIAL

British Crown Pushing War and Genocide in 2016

Pass Glass-Steagall this Month!

by David Christie

Sept. 5—In a recent discussion with colleagues, Lyndon LaRouche issued a blunt warning to the people and leaders of the United States. Speaking on the rapidly worsening financial and banking crisis, LaRouche stated that if the American people and U.S. institutions continue to *"avoid the issue of Glass-Steagall, in particular, and related issues, then the people who do that will bring their death upon themselves. You cannot afford to overlook what the issue is here. You will have a lot of dead people suddenly because they didn't pay attention."*

LaRouche's words accurately portray the stark reality of today. The entire London/Wall Street speculative financial system is at the point of implosion, and imminent chaos and death are staring us in the face.

Even if the American people choose to avert their eyes from this reality, the inevitable devastation will still come. We have been in uncharted waters for some time; exactly how far out from shore we find ourselves is unclear and the depth below unknown—but the *Götterdämmerung* of the trans-Atlantic financial system is coming. Quadrillions of dollars of unpayable derivatives and other financial contracts are now crushing the banking system. The close of the fiscal year, which ends on Sept. 30, has often been a spark for the unleashing of financial chaos and collapse in October, as occurred in 1929, 1987 and 2008. Whether or not this torrent comes in the immediate weeks ahead or at some other date in the near future, any delay in action for re-imposing the Glass-Steagall policy of Franklin Roosevelt will only make the eventual death and destruction more intense.

Some among our people and our government leaders would like to dismiss LaRouche's warnings yet once again, hoping this time he will be wrong; they would like to avoid the life and death urgency of the need to pass Glass-Steagall. Too many have allowed themselves to become mere spectators to events on stage, with many becoming self-hypnotized by the current surreal and bizarre election campaign cycle. Others who do possess some sense of the urgency of the current crisis still cite "the almighty power of Wall Street

National Archives

President Franklin Roosevelt signs the Glass-Steagall Act on June 16, 1933. Standing to his right is Sen. Carter Glass, and to his left is Rep. Henry B. Steagall, the authors of the law.

and London," and Wall's Street's control over Congress, as an excuse for their own self-imposed paralysis, saying that the passage of Glass-Steagall is impossible in the near term.

Impossible? Based on what? Three bills to reinstate Glass-Steagall are currently before the U.S. Congress, two in the House of Representatives and one in the Senate, all of them with numerous co-sponsors and bipartisan support. The demand to reinstate Glass-

Steagall is now included in the official Platforms of both the Democratic and Republican parties, as well as the Green Party platform. The reinstatement of Glass-Steagall is supported by a broad cross-section of unions, advocacy groups, and business—from the AFL-CIO and every labor union under its wing, to leading business layers up to the highest levels of international banking. Even Sandy Weill, who, during the 1990s, had championed the repeal of Glass-Steagall from his post as the head of Citibank, has endorsed its reinstatement. Many, many other business and banking leaders have echoed Weill's turn-around on the issue.

Why then do we not already have Glass-Steagall? Because the course of human history is not moved by objective facts or circumstances. There is no formula, no cumulative abacus, which will automatically provide succor at this time of crisis. Human history is created and shaped by human individuals through a subjective and personal dedication to the future of humanity. Franklin Roosevelt typified this personal responsibility and commitment to progress and to saving the people of the nation, and he organized the passage of Glass-Steagall as an integral part of that commitment, expressed by the programs of the New Deal. What is lacking today is precisely that personal commitment to the future, the willingness to fight "at all cost" for what needs to be done. It is not enough to add one's name to a piece of paper as a "co-sponsor" or to adopt a resolution so as to make a "statement." Personal accountability, courage and the willingness to fight is required from everyone who wishes to be known as a political leader, or even a citizen.

The New Financial Architecture at the G-20

An example of the necessary leadership was given by Chinese President Xi Jinping at the just-concluded G-20 Summit in Hangzhou. In his speech, wherein he specifically identified the need for a new financial architecture, i.e. banking and financial reforms that will facilitate worldwide physical economic development and poverty eradication, President Xi demonstrated the same quality of personal courage shown by Franklin Roosevelt. He spoke at length of plans for the global expansion of the New Silk Road, stressing the mutual benefit to all nations along its path, and he invited all nations to participate in this great project for human development.

For Americans and Europeans, however, the harsh reality is that Xi Jinping's call for a new financial architecture can not be accomplished without the reinstate-

ment of Glass-Steagall. Without Glass-Steagall and its related write down of the quadrillions of dollars outstanding in the global derivatives bubble, the inevitable collapse of that bubble hangs over the head of the planet like the Sword of Damocles. The parasitical gambling debt must be wiped out or it will destroy us.

The passage of Glass-Steagall is the first step toward a return to a Hamiltonian credit policy, a policy which will bring the banking system into sync with society, bringing investments for physical economic development as well as a necessary "science driver" orientation, as outlined in Lyndon LaRouche's "Four Cardinal Laws." LaRouche's Four Laws provide the principled approach to joining the New Silk Road, so that it can become the World Landbridge, as the LaRouches have envisioned for decades. This global cooperation in infrastructure will also be part of a global partnership in space exploration and joint scientific initiatives such as the needed breakthrough in thermonuclear fusion. At the G-20 Summit President Xi Jinping outlined his commitment to precisely such a policy: an economy of innovation, driven by scientific and technological progress.

Xi Jinping stated, "Scientific and technological innovation hold the key to development." China has been moving in this direction for many years. They are already taking global leadership in space exploration, and the leaders of their space program are planning for advanced missions and projects, including to the far side of the moon, a mission which is connected to the development to the development of fusion energy, through the utilization of the Helium-3 resources on the surface of the moon. The United States was planning for just such a development of lunar resources under President John F. Kennedy, but all of this was abandoned after his assassination and the subsequent policy coup d'état conducted by the forces of the British Empire.

In an echo of John F. Kennedy's phrase that a "rising tide lifts all boats," Xi Jinping stated that "In the age of economic globalization, countries are closely linked in their development and they all rise and fall together. No country could seek development on its own; and the one sure path is through coordination and cooperation. We need to realize interconnected development by promoting common development of the world economy."

President Xi also made clear that the model that China has embarked upon, is replicable by all nations— as is their coming economic upshift to an innovation economy. He cited the fact that China has pulled 700 million people out of poverty, and they intend to pull 57 million more people out of poverty by 2020—in addition to their commitment to pull other nations out of poverty.

In his speech, Xi Jinping said:

China's development has benefitted from the international community, and we are ready to provide more public goods to the international community. I have proposed the initiative of building the Silk Road Economic Belt and the 21st Century Maritime Silk Road to share China's development opportunities with countries along the Belt and Road and achieve common prosperity. Major progress has been made in launching key projects and building the economic corridors of the Silk Road Economic Belt, and the building of the 21st Century Maritime Silk Road is well underway. The Asian Infrastructure Investment Bank initiated by China has already started its positive role in regional infrastructure development ...

China's opening drive is not a one-man show. Rather, it is an invitation open to all. It is a pursuit not to establish China's own sphere of influence, but to support common development of all countries. It is meant to build not China's own backyard garden, but a garden shared by all countries.

Pass Glass-Steagall this Month

Both Russia and China have made offers to the United States to join this new paradigm, but they have all been rejected by Barack Obama. In 2014, Xi Jinping made the offer to Obama to join the New Silk Road initiative and the Asian Infrastructure and Investment Bank (AIIB). Instead, Obama unleashed a policy of military encirclement, known as the "Asia Pivot" together with the economic encirclement of the Transpacific Partnership (TPP). Russia has made similar efforts toward cooperation, such as offers to collaborate in space efforts, as well as cooperation in Arctic development and even the Bering Strait tunnel connection. All of these offers have been rejected by Obama and his

Photo/Xinhua

Chinese President Xi Jinping, leading the Sept. 4-5 G-20 summit.

handlers, and an aggressive military policy has been pursued instead. Obama's removal from office, even at this late date, would be a great signal of the intention of the United States to pursue a new direction towards peace and collaboration. Furthermore, his removal would signal the end of the subservience to the financial oligarchy that controls him.

There is no objective reason as to why we could not pass Glass-Steagall this month. Tens of millions of Americans support the reinstatement of Glass-Steagall. With the commitment by Xi Jinping at the G-20 for a new financial architecture, and the nations who support that commitment, billions globally would implicitly support the United States in adopting Glass-Steagall. It is now up to the citizens of the United States. Will we choose to commit to the future progress and development of our children and grandchildren, or will we remain obedient subjects of a dying empire? According to our Declaration of Independence, there is no choice—it is our duty to throw off such government.

With our commitment to pass Glass-Steagall this month, we will finally see the words of Franklin D. Roosevelt from his first inaugural address fully realized:

The money changers have fled from their high seats in the temple of our civilization. We may now restore that temple to the ancient truths. The measure of the restoration lies in the extent to which we apply social values more noble than mere monetary profit.

Happiness lies not in the mere possession of money; it lies in the joy of achievement, in the thrill of creative effort. The joy and moral stimulation of work no longer must be forgotten in the mad chase of evanescent profits. These dark days will be worth all they cost us if they teach us that our true destiny is not to be ministered unto but to minister to ourselves and to our fellow men.

The Saudis and 9/11: Justice Lies in The Creation of a Better Future

by Robert Ingraham and Jeffrey Steinberg

Sept. 4—On Aug. 31, 2016 former U.S. Senator Bob Graham (D-Fla.), the former head of the Senate Select Committee on Intelligence and the co-chair of the Joint Congressional Inquiry into 9/11, addressed a room full of media at the National Press Club in Washington, D.C. The Senator has been a driving force behind the recent release of the long-suppressed 28 page chapter from his report of December 2002, and he has now called for the total declassification of all of the government's investigative files on the 9/11 attacks.

The 28-page chapter from the original Joint Inquiry made clear that senior Saudi officials, starting with Prince Bandar bin-Sultan, the long-serving Saudi Ambassador to the United States, had a direct hand in supporting the 9/11 terrorists. Bandar and his wife Princess Haifa provided at least $50,000 to the hijackers al-Mihdhar and al-Hazmi, through two known Saudi intelligence agents, al-Basnan and al-Bayoumi. The paper trail is explicit, and it reaches into the upper echelons of not just the Saudi Monarchy, but the British Monarchy as well.

Colonel Lawrence Wilkerson, who served as Chief of Staff to George W. Bush's Secretary of State Colin Powell, recently told reporters that Vice President Cheney suppressed all evidence of the Saudi role in 9/11, because he was committed to blaming the World Trade Center and Pentagon attacks on Iraq's Saddam Hussein, to justify the Anglo-American invasion of Iraq in March 2003.

Senator Graham's Intervention

In his Aug. 31 Press Conference, Senator Graham detailed the fight, now underway in Florida, to declassify 80,000 pages of FBI documents on a prominent

Senator Bob Graham (D-Fla), the former head of the Senate Select Committee on Intelligence and the co-chair of the Joint Congressional Inquiry into 9/11, making a presentation at the National Press Club in Washington, D.C. Aug. 31, 2016.

LPAC TV

Saudi businessman who was tied to three of the 9/11 hijackers. A Federal Judge in Florida is now reviewing those very documents which reveal another Saudi link to 9/11, through a wealthy Saudi businessman, employed by leading Saudi princes, whose Sarasota, Florida home was frequently visited by the alleged ringleader Mohammed Atta and two other hijackers. The FBI sat on those documents for a decade, and only released them to the Judge when investigative journalists for the *Broward Bulldog* online publication found out about the Sarasota links.

Senator Graham highlighted the role of Prince Bandar bin-Sultan in providing financial and logistical support to the 9/11 hijackers in San Diego, California and reviewed some of the now-declassified details about Bandar's private security links to a leading Al-

White House/Eric Draper

President George W. Bush meets with Saudi ambassador Prince Bandar bin Sultan at the Bush ranch in Crawford, Texas, Aug. 27, 2002.

Qaeda figure, Abu Zubaida. He made a strong case for the House to immediately pass the Justice Against Supporters of Terrorism Act (JASTA), to give the 9/11 survivors and families their long-overdue day in court to actually put the Saudi Royals on trial for their complicity.

Graham spelled out three powerful reasons why the full government files on the 9/11 attack had to be made public, even fifteen years after the fact: First and foremost, the families of those killed in the 9/11 attacks, and the American people as a whole, deserved the full truth as a matter of justice; second, the national security of the United States demands a full airing of the Saudi role; and third, the cover-up of such a crime breeds cynicism in the American people, and you cannot maintain a Republic if the citizens distrust their government and cease to participate in the political process. Graham cited Benjamin Franklin, who told an inquiring citizen during the Constitutional Convention in Philadelphia that "We have given you a Republic—if you can keep it."[1]

Understanding Justice

Speaking on the topic of justice for the victims of 9/11, during the Manhattan Dialogue on Sept. 4, La-

---

1. For the full press conference by Senator Graham, see: https:// larouchepac.com/20160831/senator-bob-graham-did-saudi-royals-make-dirty-deal-bin-laden-911

Rouche PAC Policy Committee leader Diane Sare had the following to say:

To what end do we live and where is that identity? Take something like the question of what Sen. Bob Graham is doing on 9/11. How did we get to this point? Well, I would say the shift occurred in a couple of the Congressmen, namely, Congressmen Lynch from Massachusetts, and Walter Jones from North Carolina, and Massie from Kentucky, where at a certain point, it dawned on them that they should stop being afraid of what might happen to them if they decided to release the 28 Pages. And they said, publicly, "We know that we can tell the truth about this and not be prosecuted." And that was enough of a reason for Barack Obama, who had absolutely no intention in the universe of releasing those pages, to release the 28 Pages.

This was not a change in law. This was not a formal action in that sense. I think similarly, what Americans have to consider, is the way that people, including perhaps even people in this room, are thinking about the so-called election, as if voting for one of the two criminals who are current running for President on Nov. 8 has anything to do with what is going to change the affairs of mankind! Whereas, what we here are doing in these coming days on the question of securing justice is crucial, because what does justice mean in the case of the victims of 9/11? Does it really mean we have to have a lawsuit against Saudi Arabia? I don't know; it might, it might not. Putin didn't have a lawsuit against Erdogan after Turkey shot down a Russian plane, killed the pilot and put the world on the brink of thermonuclear war? No!

We don't know in what form this will occur, but we know that there is a quality whereby human beings decide to stand up and act with the intention of generating an effect which is appropriate of immortality.

In other words, there is a change which is

almost unfathomable, and is unknown to most Americans here, even though every single American is going to be affected by it, and what we are going to see coming out of these next ten days, is something very different which also depends very much upon us, in terms of communicating this with our fellow man. That's what I think we should consider: What is the nature of that change? What is the driver of it, and therefore, what does that mean for each of us, and for mankind.

Think about what happened in Berlin when the Berlin Wall came down. Was there legislation? People voted, and they decided to remove the Wall, and the Wall came down? Or, they voted, and there was an election of someone who brought the Wall down? Or they passed a rule in the parliament that the Berlin Wall was supposed to come down?

No!

You had a point, which Schiller talks about; it's in the Rütli Oath, where in the first verse, "There is a limit to a tyrant's power." And there is a certain natural principle of justice, when the population or a group of people decide that there is something more important to them about their identity than any of the physical things that enslave us; like what Socrates discussed at the end of his life about the philosopher, that you are practicing for death as a philosopher, because you try to not place so much importance on what kind of clothes you have or where you live, or all of these things that we get caught up in when we are being smaller than human beings.

Truth Does Not Have an Expiration Date

It is time for a full and honest reckoning with history. Lyndon LaRouche was on hand as the planes crashed into the World Trade Center towers on the morning of Sept. 11, 2001. Seven months prior to those attacks, LaRouche had warned that the incoming Bush-

Centennial Institute/youtube

The 46th Vice President of the United States, Dick Cheney, on Dec. 14, 2015.

Cheney Administration would look for a "Reichstag Fire" incident to go for dictatorship. On the day of the 9/11 attacks, LaRouche supporters were out on the streets of New York and many other cities around the country, warning about an imminent terrorist attack, based on evidence accumulated over the course of the summer of 2001.

The Members of the U.S. Congress, who joined with Sen. Graham and with LaRouche PAC in fighting for the release of the 28 Pages, have all said, in their own words, that the reading of those 28 Pages and the evidence they contained of the Saudi complicity in the Sept. 11, 2001 attacks, changed their view of history. Those 28 Pages merely opened the door into a much bigger scandal, which must now be fully unearthed. The families and victims of 9/11—living and dead—have the right to the truth, as do the American people.

The release of the 28 Pages was a victory for persistent public action, which forced the Obama Administration to end the nearly eight-year cover-up, which followed the eight year cover-up by Bush and Cheney.

Courage Comes from Within

Perhaps, among the reasons given by Senator Graham for the urgent necessity for the disclosure of *all* government files pertaining to the 9/11 attacks, it is his third reason—that a cover-up of this magnitude breeds cynicism in the American people, and you cannot maintain a Republic if the citizens distrust their government and cease to participate in the political process—that is the most compelling.

It is precisely this cynicism, this cowardly demoralization, that has relentlessly eaten away at the morality of the American People, and it must be reversed. Lyndon LaRouche has frequently pointed to the culpability and moral failure of the American people who witnessed the 9/11 attacks—the cold-blooded murder of thousands of our own citizens—and who failed to demand the truth; who failed to demand justice for those who died.

The issue of 9/11 today is, "Will we get justice"? Justice. Not will we get revenge, but justice in restoring our nation to a society wherein truth is the standard and people happily give their consent to be governed. A society in which citizens will no longer tolerate the crimes committed by Bush, Cheney, and Obama on a daily basis. A higher sense of national purpose is required, one which will slowly fill the souls of our citizens with a better temperament.

Between Sept. 9 and 12, a series of concerts will be performed in the New York metropolitan area commemorating the fifteenth anniversary of the 9/11 attacks. The Schiller Institute NYC Community Chorus will participate in four performances of Mozart's *Requiem*, sponsored by The Foundation for the Revival of Classical Culture.

On Sept. 2, Diane Sare reported the following:

Mozart was a supporter of the American Revolution; he was a supporter of the ideas of creating a republic, and he was murdered. His work was eliminated and his contribution to future generations was cut short. But his *Requiem* has lived on because it has a quality which is immortal, which actually embodies the question of human creativity. The choral work leading into these performances has evoked from the participants a certain kind of passion which probably was always in them. But because they have a chance to participate in something which is going to be so profound and so beautiful, and which also has a mission in the real world, they are becoming passionate again; which is, I think, something that has been very lacking. Everyone can think of conversations that you've had with your friends and neighbors about the upcoming election or almost anything; and the population has become passionless, which is why people don't act when they should or when they can.

So, I have a sense that we really are on the brink of a major breakthrough, that the United States will be a part of. Our job as Americans—in a sense—we've been given a mission that other very important leaders are saying that the United States is wanted as a valued partner in a global New Paradigm for peace and economic development. It is for us to deliver that by straightening out this criminal regime that we have.

Some have said that the lesson to be learned from 9/11 and the continuing crimes of the last fifteen years is the urgent necessity to re-establish a functioning Office of the Presidency, as such was conceived by Alexander Hamilton. This is true, but it must be understood that the Office of the Presidency is first and foremost an idea—a principle—within the minds and hearts of the people, and its existence is dependent on a commitment to the future emanating from those same people.

On Sept. 4, John Sigerson, the Conductor of the NYC Schiller Institute Community Chorus, speaking on the work going into the Living Memorial Concerts, made this observation:

And it got me to thinking about this question of justice, because I think there's still a misconception that justice is something external to you. And this is absolutely not the case. Because really to me, justice, and I think Mozart would agree with this, justice is a state of mind. It's a state of mind of the *rightness* of you, personally, participating in something *that is right*, and it's going in the right direction; and it's that warmth of soul, that passion, which *is* justice, really, if it's based on something real.

The *Requiem* mass, the core of it, is a beautiful poem. And one of the aspects of that is this idea of *lux aeterna*, which means "perpetual light"—"and let perpetual light shine upon them" [*Lux aeterna luceat eis*].

This Week in Universal History

Sept. 5—The critical weeks now before us put the question before every American (among others): how is it possible that the "little wheel" of the inmost private thoughts of the individual, succeeds in turning the "big wheel" of the historic process involving the direction and the fate of the nation and of the over seven billions of humanity as a whole, with its future, into the centuries to come?

The real story of the just-concluded China summit of the Group of 20, was that Chinese President Xi Jinping, along with Russia's Putin and the developing world led by the BRICS, plus Japan and others, forced the question of the replacement of the present financial system. They insisted that the Wall Street-London system based on gambling is heading towards another crisis, and that it must be replaced by a production-oriented system led by science and by great, leading-edge international projects: the system centered in China's New Silk Road policy, which President Xi calls, "One Belt, One Road."

The financial underpinnings of that new, human system, are provided by a series of development banks which China has helped to launch, such as the Asian Infrastructure Investment Bank (AIIB), and the New Development Bank of the BRICS.

As Helga Zepp-LaRouche noted yesterday, as the results of the G-20 summit and the preceding Vladivostok summit become apparent over the coming days, it will become clear who stands for the cause of humanity, faced with the prospect of economic annihilation, and who is obstructing. Over these days, the U.S. Congress will convene on Sept. 6, and the United Nations General Assembly on Sept 13. At the same time, the series of top-level summits will continue in Asia.

What the U.S. Congress must do when it reconvenes is to pass Glass-Steagall, for which bipartisan bills exist in both Houses of Congress. It must also act upon the facts which have been revealed by the "28 pages" of the Congressional Joint Inquiry on 9-11: to act to remove Obama for his proven deliberate coverup of Saudi (and British) responsibility for 9-11, and to force out more hidden facts on the conspiracy of the Saudis and the British, and the complicity of Bush and Cheney,— but most important, of Obama. It was our failure to remove Bush and Cheney, which gave us Obama, who is even worse. Failure to remove Obama now will give us still worse, if we are still alive to see it.

At precisely this time of urgent need for immediate political action, the leadership of the Lyndon LaRouche movement, which is located in Manhattan, is preparing for what LaRouche had called for, a "living memorial" to the victims of 9-11,— the direct victims and their families first and foremost, but also the United States and every part of the world which has been victimized by the crime and its coverup. The center of that "living memorial" will be performances of Mozart's *Requiem*, in which a great creator celebrates, not death, but the eternity of life and its mission in the face of death, through and beyond the centuries.

In and beyond this "living memorial," the

Manhattan-centered LaRouche movement is working to recreate a viable U.S. Presidency, from the same Manhattan location and through the same principles which Alexander Hamilton used in creating the original George Washington Presidency of the United States.

To address our initial question of "the little wheel" and "the big wheel": The policy of the New Silk Road began as an idea: the idea of the European Productive Triangle which Lyndon LaRouche developed in the late 1980s, and developed further, with his wife Helga, into the Eurasian Landbridge, the New Silk Road, and the World Landbridge. And the triggering event for the Chinese space program, which will bring a robotic lander to the far side of the Moon for the first time ever in 2018,— was also an idea. It was Ronald Reagan's Strategic Defense Initiative that convinced the Chinese leadership of the need for a crash science-development program including a crash space program, as will be developed in this *EIR* (see p.16). The Strategic Defense Initiative was a policy which was invented by Lyndon LaRouche out of whole cloth, and of which Reagan became convinced.

And the development banks which are being launched today, were conceived by Lyndon LaRouche in the 1970s, when they were proposed before the United Nations General Assembly by Guyana's distinguished Foreign Minister, the late Fred Wills.

As the great Russian scientist Vladimir Vernadsky showed in the first half of the Twentieth Century, human noësis, or creative reason, is the most powerful force in the universe. There is no power which equals that of the human mind in the mode of creative discovery.